D0955578

Things I Wish I'd Known Sooner...

Things I Wish I'd Known Sooner...

Jaroldeen Edwards

Deseret Book Company
Salt Lake City, Utah

Library of Congress Cataloging-in-Publication Data

Edwards, Jaroldeen.
    Things I wish I'd known sooner : personal discoveries of a mother
  of twelve / by Jaroldeen Edwards.
      p. cm.
    ISBN 0-87579-515-3
    1. Mothers—United States—Psychology. 2. Wives—United States—
Psychology. 3. Women—United States—Psychology. 4. Motherhood—
Religious aspects—Mormon Church. I. Title
HQ759.E28 1991
306.874'3—dc20   90-26623
                                                   CIP

Printed in the United States of America

10   9   8   7   6   5   4   3   2   1

Contents

Contents

Preface

This is not a "how-to" book.

It is not a book with tidy answers to untidy questions.

It is not a "perfect person" book.

It is not an easy book.

What this book is, is a book of personal discoveries, expressed as precious, albeit one-sided, conversations we might have had through the years, as friends. Our conversations would probably have touched on the full spectrum of our lives — intellectual knowledge, scriptural insights, personal anecdotes, observations from other cherished and admired friends, shared housekeeping hints, and all of the glorious, myriad "stuff" (as Shakespeare called it) of which our dreams are made.

Women's conversations are splendid things — diverse, profound, humorous, complex, and vivid. But if women's conversations are diverse, it is only because they reflect the fact that we, as women, are diverse. Our lives are individual and kaleidoscopic, filled with changing seasons and unique, personal challenges. By accepting, understanding, and learning from this shared and wondrous diversity, we gain greater joy, truer purpose, and a wider vision of the endless chain of our own possibilities.

The conversation of true friends, properly heard — without envy, defensiveness, false barriers, comparisons, or criticism — is good for the soul.

As I began to write this book I remembered something my mother-in-law once told me. She was talking about her own mother, Caroline Romney Eyring, and she said, "Mother was an impatient cook, but, as a result, she made wonderful pies." I was a new bride and the comment startled me, since I regarded pie making as postdoctoral cooking. I could see no possible relationship between a cook's impatience and the ability to produce something as complex and delectable as a pie.

"You see," Weston's mother went on to explain, "the less you handle pie crust, the more tender and flaky it is."

I think that what is true of pie crust is true of conversation as well. The more directly our thoughts come from our hearts, the more tender and true they will be.

So I have rolled out my pie crust . . .

Acknowledgments

With abiding gratitude . . .

To my parents, Charles and Julia Asplund, who taught me to love life, the gospel, and the written word.

To my friends, cherished, but too numerous to mention, who have decorated and illuminated my life.

To my editor, Eleanor Knowles, whose gifts of insight and discernment make the best, better.

To great writers whose words themselves bring light.

To my blessed children, Marianna, Julia, Catherine, Charles, Christine, Robin, Carolyn, Weston, Robert, William, Jaroldeen, and Patricia, more precious than words, more valued than words can say, more dear than the heart can hold.

To my beloved husband, Weston Eyring Edwards, counselor, friend, adviser, enabler, supporter, teacher, lover, mentor, example — and all in all.

To all who have made my life so rich with joy — and who put up with this decidedly unfinished woman.

Light—more light!
—Last words of
Wolfgang Amadeus Mozart

An Illuminated Life

Standing in the Huntington Library in San Marino, California, surrounded by glass-enclosed display cases filled with rare parchment and vellum manuscripts from the fourteenth and fifteenth centuries, I pause at a softly lighted case containing an open volume. Each letter, in deep-black ink, is a work of art—straight and exquisite in detail and execution. The Latin or Old English words flow together in sentences indecipherable to my unskilled mind.

At the beginning of each page, one glorious letter, splashed with gold, radiant with scrolls, flowers, carmine, and royal blue, stands like a beacon. Down the center of the page, in the margins, and across the bottom of the manuscript are minutely detailed illustrations. Suddenly, in the colorful mosaic of design, I discern knights and ladies on horseback, their miniature costumes capturing forever — as fresh as this moment — their moment in time.

And now my eye discerns the meaning of the black letters running together, and I read: "Whan that Aprill with his shoures soote . . . " Ah yes, I see! *The Canterbury Tales!*

The illustrations and decorations in these precious manuscripts are called *illuminations.* Patient medieval scholars, artists, and copyists highlighted their work with pure gold, the rarest of inks and dyes, and the most delicate and elaborate designs. They *illuminated* for beauty; *illuminated* for moments of quick and true understanding; *illuminated* to pierce tedium and apathy with sudden, magnificent vision. With their illuminations they turned the humble pages of their repetitive task into treasured works of lasting art.

A number of years ago I accompanied my husband on a business trip to Barbados. It was an enormously exciting trip, the first time I had ever been outside the continent of North America and the first time I had ever been to an island.

The journey involved several plane connections, the final one in a bitter snowstorm in New York. By late afternoon we arrived on the island. My fantasy of what a Caribbean island was going to be like was a cross between the paintings of Gauguin and old movies starring Bob Hope and Dorothy Lamour — palm trees swaying, the scent of frangipani (whatever that was), flowers, lush ferns, and the ocean lapping at my feet.

As we were herded off our airplane onto an open tarmac, all we could see was empty sky and other airplanes. We were hurried into the terminal and crowded into small English-made taxis. With luggage piled on our laps, we began our dizzying ride to our hotel.

Our taxi drove along a narrow, winding road (which I later learned went down the center of the small island) between tall stands of sugarcane ready to be harvested. For nearly an hour we sped along, passing other taxis, seeing an occasional small house or a windmill, but for the most part green fields banked the road, and it felt as though we were driving through a long tunnel.

Finally we arrived at our hotel, where we were driven into a small courtyard and greeted in a tiny, vine-shrouded villa by a courtly gentleman. He called for a bellman, who took our bags and invited us to follow him down a twisting path that was overhung with flowering shrubs. Finally we stopped at the door of our cottage. As we entered our room, the door closed behind us and we stood blinking in the darkness. I could hear the bellman walk across the floor to the opposite wall and deposit our suitcases on a stand.

Confused and weary, I stood by the door, waiting for my eyes to grow accustomed to the darkness. I had been in this paradise for over an hour, and all I had experienced was disappointment. Nothing was what I had dreamed it would be. Nothing made sense. I didn't even know where I was — somewhere on an island in the middle of an ocean, neither of which I was even sure existed at this point.

Just then the doorman pressed a latch, and with a dramatic sweep of his hands he threw open some floor-to-ceiling shutters that we had not discerned in the darkness. As suddenly as though he had turned on a searchlight, the room was bathed in glorious light, and there before us, where only darkness had existed one second before, was the splendid tropical sun shining in a sky of burnished turquoise. And stretching as far as my eyes could see was the endless sapphire Caribbean, the froth of its lacy-white surf lapping up to edge of a dazzling beach. The far wall of our room was made of glass with sliding doors, and the great window had been there all the time. While I had stood in darkness, confused and disappointed, in front of my very eyes, with only a thin barrier separating me from the knowledge of it, was the whole of eternity.

Illumination. That is what it is all about. Those brief moments in the darkness and confusion of our daily lives when a word, a thought, an action throws open the shutters, and for a brief instant, through an uncovered window, we glimpse a portion of forever.

Know thyself...
The glory, jest, and riddle of the world.
— Alexander Pope

Chapter One

Magic Windows of Light

I was the guest speaker at a women's conference. After the meetings an energetic, no-nonsense sort of a young woman came up to me, looked me squarely in the eye, and said, "You know, Sister Edwards, when I heard you were going to be our speaker, I almost decided not to come."

Needless to say, she had my instant attention. But before I could respond, she continued: "I didn't know you, of course, and I had never heard you speak, but when I read your biography in the publicity materials the stake sent out—that you have twelve children, and have published five novels, and have served as ward Relief

Society president, and have a wonderful marriage, and on and on—well, all I could think was, 'Oh no! Here comes another of those women with a perfectly organized house and brilliant children, who is successful in the world, and who is coming to tell me how easily she does it all!'

"To be perfectly honest, Sister Edwards, I didn't want to hear it—not when I'm struggling just to manage my four children and help my husband with our small business. My house is never organized, my children can drive me wild, and it's hard for me to find time to prepare a decent Primary lesson. I couldn't stand the thought of spending a precious morning-off listening to some impossibly successful woman tell me what I'm doing wrong."

She paused, and for the first time she smiled at me. Her smile illuminated her face as though she had stepped from a dark room into the sunlight. She grasped my hand and continued warmly, "But, Sister Edwards, after hearing you speak I feel very close to you. Why, you are so ordinary that nobody could hate you!"

Ordinary. That was one of the best compliments I had ever received because it was more than a compliment. It was actually a gift of knowledge and insight. Without realizing it, this woman had made a profound observation about our mortal experience and eternal spiritual relationship. (I had obviously succeeded in communicating to her the fact that my home was not always organized, that I had very real children, and that I, too, struggled to find both time and identity.) However, the concept implied in her words went further than a comfortable recognition of my imperfections. She had meant her comments to be a deep, sincere, and specific compliment. I loved it, and it spurred me to contemplate the idea of ordinariness in an entirely new light.

My thoughts reinforced my already deep conviction about human relationships. I have always felt that although the circumstances of individual lives — personalities, patterns, abilities, place — may be dramatically different, still, in meaningful ways, we are all much alike. Those things we have in common are far greater than those things that divide us. Only when we are wise enough, trusting enough, loving enough, and generous enough to see through the outward trappings of another person's life — to see instead the bedrock of shared needs, desires, struggles, and spiritual aspirations — are we able to truly recognize one another. Then we can feel more comfortable with our own lives and more appreciative and accepting of others.

In such moments of insight, in a brief window of light, we see and understand that we are all gloriously ordinary. I say *gloriously* because the most common characteristic shared by ordinary people is that each one has an individual life that is splendidly unique and in some wonderful and mysterious way extraordinary. One of the great miracles of Heavenly Father is that he somehow made each of us extraordinary and ordinary at the same time.

As we begin to explore this fascinating dichotomy, discovering both the eternal and unchanging principles of truth that apply to all and the incredible sweep and complexity of individual challenge, we begin to comprehend the magnificent harvest of hidden treasures of knowledge that have been promised and that lie within the scope of our own personal lives. One of the primary goals of mortality is to learn. Mortality serves as our laboratory; our own individual life is our learning tray; and the lives of others can be like a resource library.

Learning trays were given to early students of science. Each student had an individual tray with an array of artifacts and specimens on it. The challenge was for the scholar to discover scientific truths through personal study, experimentation, and observations based upon his or her own particular tray. Tutors, other students, libraries, and other resources were available if the pupil chose to use them. Those students who succeeded quickly developed methods and systems of inquiry. They were eager and persistent. They focused on the tray given to them, but asked questions and gained knowledge from others. They observed others and learned from them. Using creativity, trial and error, and enthusiasm for the process, they remained motivated. Sometimes, in the midst of dutiful effort, they would have a brief moment of surprised light when they would suddenly grasp an elusive truth. Such moments came unexpectedly—but in the midst of the fray. The least productive students spent their time gazing at their classmates' trays, wishing they had gotten the nautilus shell, the turquoise rock, or the ant farm.

We must hunger and thirst after knowledge, which is the real treasure, and when we do, we become more grateful for individual life, for it is the means to that end. True principles, once identified, are true, and it does not matter the tray by which they are discovered. Molecular structure can be learned from a daisy or from a snail.

Thus it is that the mother in Lapland who gently rocks

her child to sleep shielding his eyes from a never-setting sun, or the Bedouin mother who feeds her child goat's-milk yogurt in the blazing heat, or the Andean mother who straps her child close to her body so he may sleep as she climbs the mountain path in the thin, cold air — each may learn the identical knowledge of love.

I remember vividly the day my eighth child was placed in my arms. Why then? Why the eighth time? Not a new thought or a new feeling — but one that I suddenly felt and knew in that instant so profoundly that I shook with the knowledge. As I held that dear baby, he opened his eyes and looked at me, and in that ordinary moment, deep within his eyes, as though I were actually looking through a telescope I saw the whole vision of eternity. I gasped. I cannot describe it any better than that. For a brief instant, in the direct and silent intelligence of those brand-new eyes from which gazed a spirit as everlastingly old and young as my own, I saw a microcosm of premortal life; the love of my Heavenly Father, the mature soul in that infant's body, and the truth of our binding and eternal covenants. I felt I had been privileged to look through his eyes to see a glimpse of heaven. For just one brief instant, all the walls had fallen away.

Later that night I wrote the following words:

> A child's eyes are the cathedral of a mother's soul:
> Through them she worships flawlessly.
> In them she sees eternity.

Knowledge may come in many ways, but it is those sudden, unexpected moments of insight that particularly intrigue me, those moments in our questing when a veil is suddenly torn from our eyes and we see clearly. I am fascinated, for example, to know that the principles of physics have always existed, since the creation of the world, and are demonstrated daily in the workings of the earth. Through the centuries, how many apples do you suppose had fallen right in front of people's eyes—and yet no one saw them? Then Isaac Newton observed a falling apple with a vision that somehow penetrated its simplicity and dailiness, and because he truly saw, the world was changed forever. He identified a truth that had always been there, just waiting to be seen—universal truth, but discovered through individual experience in an individual life.

A number of years ago, when we contemplated placing our children in a Montessori school, I decided to make a study of the life of Maria Montessori. At the turn of the century, Maria worked with mentally handicapped children in the slums of Rome. There she discovered the great principle of learning upon which she based her schools. She found that if children are placed in an environment completely filled with learning opportunities, they will gain knowledge inadvertently, at their own pace, in their own patterns.

Everything in the Montessori classroom is designed to have the potential for teaching a concept. The height of the windows, the squares on the floor, the places where things are kept—everything is designed for teaching sequencing, motor control, spatial concepts, categorization, and other essential skills.

One example I found especially creative was that all the little girls in Madame Montessori's boarding school wore dresses with buttons from neck to hem and were taught to button and unbutton their dresses in precise order. Thus, the natural and repetitive function of daily dressing became an automatic learning experience in manual dexterity, sequencing, and patterning.

As I read I had a burst of personal insight. "This is the very principle," I thought to myself, "upon which the Lord has designed this earth and our experience in mortality." I could visualize our earthly existence as a vast, splendidly designed classroom in which every single thing both abstract and concrete is designed as a means for us to gain knowledge. I could also see that for the most part we play, work, and interact like the children in a classroom, largely unaware of the bounty of knowledge at our fingertips.

Our lack of full comprehension is not an indictment. It is one of the realities of our mortal limitations. We live through this span of existence with the veil drawn so that knowledge must be gained through living with faith, through keeping the commandments, and through dependence upon revelation and the guidance of the Holy Ghost.

Not until the earth is celestialized will it become a Urim and Thummim to reveal all the vast knowledge it holds in store. At that time we shall see clearly, as though through a crystal, and through that crystal the mysteries that the earth has to teach will unfold before the righteous as a scroll. The earth will then become its own translator.

Paul, in explaining this to the Corinthians, alluded to the great knowledge that lies about us: "For now we see through a glass, darkly; but then face to face: now I know

in part; but then shall I know even as also I am known."
(1 Corinthians 13:12.) But the wonderful part is that even
though it is through a dark glass, we do see! Every once
in a while, even in this telestial phase of our eternal
journey, disguised in the ordinary substance of our daily
experience, we catch a glimpse of the knowledge that lies
all about us. In such brief moments we are blessed to
see with Urim and Thummim eyes. Pure knowledge sends
a sudden ray and we learn a truth that gives meaning,
substance, and beauty to our lives. We can develop eyes
that will see those moments more clearly, and the wisdom
to remember them more vividly.

It is some of these glimpses of surprised light in my
own life that I would like to share with you. James Joyce
calls such moments *epiphanies.* I rather like that word. It
has a rich, important sound to it—and a touch of exaltation
as well. A word like *epiphany,* however, cannot take itself
too seriously, because it has kind of a homely sound, too,
like *piffle* or *funny.* I like that because moments of en-
lightenment can be pretty down-to-earth and humorous.
Epiphany literally means a flash of pure light and understanding—one of those rare moments when nature,
people, emotions, and spirit coalesce to create an instant
of total comprehension.

Tennyson understood this. In "Flower in the Crannied
Wall" he wrote:

> I pluck you out of the crannies,
> I hold you here, root and all, in my hand,
> Little flower—but *if* I could understand
> What you are, root and all, and all in all,
> I should know what God and man is.

So there you are! The things of eternity revealed in the humdrum. The extraordinary, flowering in the most ordinary.

I have gathered, like a bouquet of memory, some of my own moments of epiphany, gleaned from my own learning tray. These are certainly not all glorious lessons about celestial things. Some of my epiphanies are as simple and valuable as the way my ten-year-old daughter taught me how to make cookies more efficiently. (I have to confess that I believe the principles of truth apply to cookie making as much as to a better understanding of the eternal nature of womanhood.)

Truth and knowledge seem to have an incredible gamut of subjects. We cannot be saved in ignorance, but sometimes learning comes in unexpected ways: from the eyes of our children, the words of a friend, or the hum of a washing machine.

Light from this window:

The most ordinary things can become windows of light.

The time to be happy is now,
The place to be happy is here,
The way to be happy is to make others so.
— Robert Green Ingersoll

Chapter Two

Prime Time

I don't know why you would listen to somebody who missed her own prime! Because I did. I just plain missed it. I don't know if it occurred at two o'clock some morning when I was too busy rocking a colicky baby to notice, or if it whizzed by me one day when I was dozing in a long PTA meeting, or if it sneaked past me while I was waxing the kitchen floor. Whenever, and wherever it happened, I cannot tell you, but I do remember the *exact* moment when I recognized it had gone past me without my even noticing.

Like every other well-brought-up young woman, I was

raised to believe that life was a crescendo. "Do everything right—eat your cereal, curl your hair, study, exercise, be sweet, and follow The Plan (although I was never too clear exactly what the 'Plan' was), and someday your life will be a success. You will reach 'Happily-Ever-After' and remain in that desirable—if somewhat nebulous—state for the rest of your life."

I confidently expected that the time in my life would come when everything would be just as it was supposed to be—perfect. Of course, life kept getting in the way, but that didn't discourage me, since I knew that it would take a lot of years of effort and growth to reach the dreamed-of peak. I was patient—and besides, I was having an absolutely wonderful time on the way to getting there.

When my oldest child was ready to begin kindergarten, we lived in student housing in Cambridge, Massachusetts. My husband was a graduate student, and we lived in the rather run-down but old-world charm of Holden Green. The townhouse-style apartments were filled with young couples like us, with lots and lots of children. It was a small, enclosed world of husbands who were graduate students and mothers who lived on pennies and cared for their babies. It was happy times and hopes and friendships and laughter and eyes filled with tomorrows.

When Marianna was due to start kindergarten, we registered her in the Harvard preschool. It was a prestigious institution and we could barely afford the tuition, but we wanted her to have the very best. Since she was already the oldest of five children, we were determined to start this education business just right.

We lived in the heart of Cambridge, within walking

distance of church and school, and did not have a car. I remember walking Marianna to school that first day. The September sun was like sifted gold, and the beech trees lining the narrow streets were radiant in the beginning of the autumn colors. Each magnificent old house along the walk was like a story waiting to be told. I was pushing the stroller with the baby and my toddler in it, and the other three children skipped beside me. We were all full of the sheer delight of the sights and sounds around us and the excitement of Marianna's first day of school.

When we arrived at the school I stood outside for a moment and watched the other children arriving. Most of them were the children of professionals in the community. They were driven up to the school in Mercedes and shining station wagons and sports cars. Their mothers, most of them women in their thirties and forties, with hair impeccably set, beautiful suits from Peck and Peck, shining shoes—all looked like magazine models to me.

I stood there with my children playing around my legs. My hair was wind-blown from the walk, and I was wearing jeans and sneakers. The stroller looked the worse for wear, and I was frazzled from trying to keep the little ones out of the street and away from the cars. The contrast with those cool, controlled women was rather dramatic.

As I kissed Marianna good-bye and walked home to put the children down for their naps, I thought to myself, "It doesn't matter. Those are all older women, and their husbands are well-along in their careers. They don't have a lot of little children at home. They certainly aren't living on a student budget, and so they have time and money to spend on clothes and things. That's exactly how I'll be someday. In the meantime I'm just going to love being young and busy."

The years passed. My darling husband, Weston, graduated from graduate school and Marianna graduated from kindergarten. We moved through the years with Weston's work from Chicago to New Jersey to Los Angeles to Scarsdale, New York.

Two months after moving to Scarsdale, we had our twelfth child, Patricia. I was in my early forties now, with twelve children and an old colonial house with apple trees and all the children in the neighborhood in my front yard. Twenty years had passed as quickly as though they had been one short autumn day.

It was time for school to start again, and I had a child beginning kindergarten. My high school students drove themselves to school, and I packed the remaining seven children in our blue van. This battered, inelegant vehicle had taken Scouts camping, had moved dozens of fellow Latter-day Saints, and had taken us across the country more times than I cared to count.

We drove to the lovely, English-style brick school, with its gentle draping of ivy. It was a glorious fall day, with the trees blushing yellow and red and the winding streets of Scarsdale lined with gracious homes. I had been waxing the kitchen floor that morning and had hurriedly plucked the baby from her high chair for the drive to school. With the crying baby on my hip and two toddlers clinging to my legs, I took Robert into the school to settle him in his classroom.

As I left the school I prepared to climb into the old blue van when something caught my attention. All around me I saw *young* mothers, in their twenties, bringing their immaculate children to school. They were driving Mercedes and shining station wagons. Their hair was shining and smooth and their clothes were Country Chic—shining loafers, tweed skirts, and expensive sweaters. I stood and looked down at myself. Somehow, somewhere, sometime along the way I had become the *older* mother—and here I was, still in jeans and sneakers, with a slightly battered vehicle and young children clinging to my legs!

Shaking my head, with a rueful smile I looked down at my three-month-old baby lying in her car seat. She gave me a toothless grin, and a little dribble of milk ran down her chin. Her eyes were the color of the sky, and she looked at me as though we had known one another forever.

"Shucks, honey," I said with a philosophical shrug of my shoulders, "somewhere between Cambridge and Scarsdale I missed my prime!"

What made this moment so enlightening for me was that I suddenly realized that for years and years I had not even thought of the concept of a prime of life. My life had been so full of meaningful challenges, staggering amounts of work, living, complex relationships, and a growing focus and awareness of eternal goals that my young, simplistic view of an ultimate ideal mold into which I would eventually fit had long since lost any validity in my life. As a matter of fact, the best thing I had discovered in adult life was that I get to choose my own patterns, to put first the things that matter the most to me and to my family. Yet I had to stop and wonder how much of my sense of self and my list of priorities had been affected through the years by the expectations of society and a preconceived notion of the things that would spell success in the eyes of others.

The scariest thing we can do is to let society, or the opinion of others, or a television-sitcom mentality decide for us where our time, efforts, emotions, and money should be spent. Is prime time only when fresh bread is taken from the oven? Is prime time only when we can afford Guess jeans and a BMW? Is prime time only when our days follow a neatly prescribed pattern in our Franklin Planner? Is prime time only when our husband's work is satisfying and rewarding? Is prime time only when we are serving in a position that is visible and important?

I do not think so. As a matter of fact, many of these things, fine as they are, can be barriers to what are truly our own personal prime experiences.

Outward measures of perceived success reflect preconceived ideas patterned by society and the expectations — or the concept of the expectations — of others. We cannot blame anyone but ourselves if we are influenced by these visions of mythical ideals, however, because it is our own responsibility to evaluate and choose wisely from all that is around us those things which will give our lives value and meaning.

The difficult thing for women in creating a life that they can feel is prime is that they must make so many choices between things that are good. For example, it is a good thing to bake bread, but for many women this simply is not the best or wisest use of their precious time. We cannot do everything, all the time, all at once. We can, through the years, do many things, at different times, one at a time. It is important to see choices as opportunities, not as frustrations. It is even more important to believe in our free agency and the opportunity and responsibility to make those choices.

When we go into debt to purchase something with the purpose of impressing others, we let others make the choice, and do we create a moment of prime-of-success or months of penury? By contrast, some of the choicest times in our lives may well be times of sickness, poverty, and uncertainty, when all the deepest and most profound resources of our marriage and our individual strength will be tested. The value of such times will be visible to no one but ourselves.

Who has the right to tell us what is prime in our own lives? Once we recognize the fact that we are the only ones who can do so, we become free to develop and relish the prime factors that exist in our own personal experience.

Our life can enter a stage of true personal discovery and the kind of freedom from worldly preconceptions that Sir Henry Bessemer, inventor of the process of steel making, exulted in when he said: "I had an immense advantage over many others dealing with the problem inasmuch as I had no fixed ideas derived from long-established practice to control and bias my mind, and did not suffer from the general belief that whatever is, is right."

My wonderful conclusion on that long-ago night in Scarsdale, as I put my children to bed, kissed them good-night, and looked at my rumpled, bumbling house full of things to do—some of which I loved doing and some of which I would procrastinate as long as I decently could—was that I had not missed my prime at all. Oh yes, I had missed that prime pictured in the magazines; I would never be young and svelte, with coordinated towels (although I solve that problem in another chapter), a perpetually clean refrigerator, and coordinated children. But I had not missed my prime—my own personal, wonderful, wouldn't-change-it-for-the-world prime. I had been living it every day all through the years.

To anyone else my life probably just looked noisy, confusing, disorganized, untidy, and improbable, but the point is that no one else gets to put the value on our life—no one but Heavenly Father and ourselves. To me all the years, even the hard ones, had been prime. Better than prime: choice.

Light from this window:

When we live our lives dealing with things that really matter, the things that don't matter—don't.

Waste not your Hour, nor in the vain pursuit
Of This and That endeavour...
                              — Omar Khayyám

Chapter Three

A Full House

reamble: It would be hard to explain to women who did not live through it what it was like to be a woman, a wife, and a mother in the 1970s. There was a harsh, divisive, strident movement in the ranks of feminism. The media, society, schools, universities, newspapers, magazines, and the voices of highly visible men and women proclaimed that there were too many children in the world and that women should not allow themselves to be chained to the home, husbands, or children. It was the "me" generation, with women crying "my turn" the loudest of anyone.

Zero Population Growth, the Population Boom, and

the Feminine Mystique were all catch phrases under which a mix of lies, personal angers, unproven theories, and destructive attitudes were packaged and sold to an impressionable generation of women.

There is no question that some good came from this upheaval. Women's issues were opened, discussed, and acknowledged, and many rights were established. New directions became possible. But many bitter legacies from that decade linger still: a devaluing of children both in society and in personal lives, diminished respect for the traditional roles of women, the proliferation of abortion, divorce in epidemic proportions, and a polarization of men and women.

It was a time of what I like to call "The Big Lie," when slogans masqueraded as ideas, and propaganda and emotion were disguised to look like thoughtful analysis. The tasks of homemaking and motherhood were demeaned as drudgery while *jobs* were referred to as *careers* and glorified out of all proportion—certainly with very little relationship to the realities of most jobs. Few women were able to refrain from being influenced by the pervasive anti-child and anti-family-role themes.

In the disguise of freeing women, this new movement was actually brilliantly forging new "manacles of the mind" (as John W. Gardner, the author of *Self-Renewal*, calls it). There are, of course, many ways to manacle minds, but none so cleverly used in the decade of the seventies as the catchy phrase masquerading as a responsible and established truth. For example, almost always when writers or speakers referred to the role of motherhood they would characterize it by the phrase "dirty diapers and dirty dishes." Now that's smart strategy. In a single phrase they had captured two of the universally necessary but unappealing activities of mothering, had stripped motherhood to what they (and many others) considered to be its lowest common denominator, and by so doing had neatly denigrated the role and diminished the mother and the child by reducing them to menial functions.

It didn't work on me because I understood that mothering was infinitely more than any ridiculous catch phrase. I also knew something about diapering a child that none of those clever feminists knew—or could probably even understand. I refuse to let my mind be manacled—and certainly not by women who don't even know what they are talking about. If there is one thing in this world upon which I am an expert, it is probably changing diapers. When I was confronted with this ad-campaign level of thinking, I decided to evaluate for myself what it really means to change diapers. Is it really a demeaning activity for a Phi Beta Phi college graduate?

To begin with, there is no question that caring for an infant is a godlike endeavor. Without the thoughtful, gentle care of a loving adult, babies die. They die of starvation, disease, filth, and emotional neglect. There is no alternative. Babies must be cared for—and well cared for—or there is no continuation of life on this planet. It is the single imperative of continued mortal existence. When we care for a fragile infant, we deal with matters of life and death; there is nothing demeaning or unimportant in anything we do.

So we come to the changing of diapers, an inevitable

interface of caretaker and child. Of course it is a distasteful task, but in it a bonding of service, of love, and of cleanliness. It is much more than that, however. When we change a child's diaper, it is necessary to look that baby squarely in the eye; to talk to it; to charm it; to woo it; to distract it; to entertain it—to do everything within our power to keep the child content, happy, and entertained while we perform the tricky task. So it is that changing diapers requires a mother, several times a day, to interact with her baby, face to face, with all the charm and delight of which she is capable.

T. Barry Brazelton, a great pediatric authority, discovered a direct correlation between the effectiveness of mothers and the frequency of eye-to-eye contact. Changing diapers is prime eye-to-eye time. Physically and emotionally such daily activities as feeding, bathing, and diapering become the taproots of the eternal relationship of mother and child. These functions contain the quality time of infancy. I have witnessed a mother diapering her baby while being so charming, adorable, vivid, and exuberant that she and the child rang with laughter like golden bells. Only those who have never analyzed the value and purpose of such activities can look at them with contemptuous eyes.

Some time ago a journal published for the Mormon audience was preparing an issue devoted to women's concerns and many of the difficult and valid problems that were part of the whirlwind. I was asked by the editors to write an essay on motherhood. We were in the thick of the seventies and the women's movement, and to write at that time in praise of motherhood—especially of a large family—was a little like being asked to write an essay on democracy for a newspaper in China. I had been a tournament debater in college, and my natural instinct was to write a defense of motherhood. On point after point I planned to best the adversary.

As I wrote and rewrote the essay, in my mind I came to a firm conviction that I still hold: There are true principles upon which one must base the decisions of one's life. When we receive blessings it is by obedience to true principles. There are many true principles, however, and many different decisions can be derived from them, and each person has the right to choose for himself or herself. I cannot judge for anyone else.

In the end, I decided that all I could do was write the truth about my own experience and feelings—tell others what I felt about the joys and challenges of my life, and let them take from my words whatever might be of value and truth to them. So, rather than a long defense of children, motherhood, and apple pie, I wrote, as honestly as I could, the account of a day in my life. I had just had my eleventh child and we were living in California at the time. What I hoped was that I could show, rather than advocate, how I felt about my profession. When the article was published the editors wrote and told me that "people who read your essay either loved it or hated it—there was no in between." (Did I mention that women were polarized in the 1970s?)

Here are some thoughts from that essay, which includes many of the windows of light I have discovered managing a house full of children.

A Full House

I wake up in the morning to the sound of my husband's voice. But it is not really an awakening; rather it is a continuing. For night as we used to know it no longer comes to our home. There is a lull in activity, yes; but in the way of our youth, when night and sleep were a total experience that blocked the chain of days, a precious all-in-one piece of unconsciousness, an ending and a for-getting — in that sense night does not come. Even in sleep there is a consciousness of caring, a wakefulness that tests the murmur of the house through the darkened hours. The hum of the refrigerator, a last dryer of clothes with one clonking sneaker, water flushing, a cough, children padding on pajamaed feet through the always lighted halls, requests for drinks, solace from bad dreams, or a short diagnosis of unidentified aches.

Sometimes I open my eyes in response to an eerie sense of presence and see a face an inch from mine, staring. Child standing, me lying, eye to eye. "I can't sleep," and then the blissful snuggle in. Or there will be a gentle arising to the surface of sleep, a sudden awareness of silence, a listening ... listening ... listening ... and set-tling back to sleep in the wonder and reassurance of our burgeoned home.

Not yet six in the morning. My husband is shaving and calls over the running water — something from the train of his thoughts. He assumes that I am (a) awake and (b) fully aware of his mental preamble, even though he knows that we have an unspoken agreement: "I never wake to the sound of an alarm, and he never wakes to the crying of a baby." He cannot resist this brief empty piece of time — no more can I, so I rouse and prop in bed and we continue the delicious conversation of our marriage. Fifteen minutes. Then up, making the bed, hair, slippers, robe, and a quick glance at our baby sleeping like a moist rose. Such beauty in our cluttered bedroom!

Morning husbands are so elegant. He comes from the dressing room in his starched white shirt, bright tie, polished shoes, face shining from shower and shave. All the beautiful odors, soap, shaving lotion, starch, and the masculine smell of his suit, mingle in that early morning embrace.

Breakfast with our seminary daughters is eggnog, toast, and orange juice. Never time for more. The girls hurtle into the kitchen, shoes in hand, long shining hair, books a-clutter, hunting for gym suits or brushes or pens. Their day fresh and new. I never get used to seeing them grown so tall and beautiful. I love their becoming, but I miss the little girls gone. It is a constant challenge to keep my relationship to them in the proper balance since it must change and develop as they do. Too often the childhood mother rises to the surface and makes a flat evaluation: "Change those stockings!" "Skirt's too short." "Please take a sweater." "Do you have your homework and lunch?" Compromises reached, plans exchanged. As they fling out the door, with coats, books, and purses, I give each a brief kiss and a careful compliment, the ritual that says, "I love you. Hurry home."

Then one last apostrophe of time with my husband. Six-thirty A.M. He looking like Brooks Brothers and me like the Earth Mother.

The next half hour is my own sweet time. It's gorgeous to read in a still-sleeping house, prepare a church assignment, or spend quiet minutes with an early-awakened baby. At seven I must be fully dressed with makeup and hair done, ready for the official day of the family to begin. The children are wakened, first time cheerfully, second time firmly, and, if a third time is necessary, sharply.

I dress the preschool children and babies in my bedroom. This bedroom is the hub of our home in the morning and evening. Here I keep a drawer with the stockings for the entire family. This serves two purposes. Naturally it saves a lot of sorting time, but it also makes it necessary for each child to come from the corners of the house to this room to complete dressing. I can make all the necessary checks — hair, teeth, clothes, homework, and morning chores. The stocking drawer is a siphon and it draws all the early-morning family to me while I am busy changing diapers, tying shoes, and snapping trousers for the four youngest.

Breakfast and lunches are prepared with practiced swiftness. Simple meals. Bowls of hot cereal, milk, and oranges. Lunches crackling in brown paper sacks with each name in marker pen — Catherine, Charles, Christine, Robin, Carolyn. Sandwiches all the same ("Sorry you don't like cheese, Robin; I'll make peanut butter tomorrow." Carolyn says she doesn't like peanut butter and we all laugh. "Tuna on Wednesday!" I promise.), cookies, apples, and milk money. Gathered around the kitchen table, the children and I cram these last minutes with talking, facts, ideas, compliments, appointments, schedules. Family prayer and momentary silence as they start to eat.

The clock is inexorable. So is the school bus. Again at the door the farewells. My cheek is kissed and I forget to wipe off the cereal and milk. Midday I will sometimes touch my cheek and find it still sticky.

Catherine's junior high starts later and so we do dishes and have a rare private talk. She practices flute or piano and, long dark hair bouncing, strides off to school. It would be wonderful to have eleven children and have each an only child.

Bless Sesame Street! That psychedelic learning feast! My three little boys sit in a rapt row. Fifteen minutes of hard exercise for me while they watch; the misery of middle-age, eleven children, and all that car-driving is that muscle tone is no longer inherent—it has to be earned.

I fill the sink to bathe the baby. It is a time of savoring. Maybe it has taken me all these children to appreciate how short these first months are. The glories of a new baby are beyond description. Hardly mortal! I revel in this tactile, subtle, exquisite, and complex experience. One unexpected bonus of motherhood is the visual beauty. I am enchanted by the sights of my children, the tones of skin, the clear eyes, the grace, the curve of hand and cheek—to see them racing across the back lawn in a certain slant of light.

At about ten o'clock the baby is cared for and the discretionary part of the day begins. There is no one to tell me what I must do, only my own sense of responsibility and achievement. People often ask me how I manage with such a large family and I reply, "By a simple method of selective neglect." Which is just a way of saying that I manage through a system of compelling priorities.

My present life as a mother has three profound purposes. (This aside from the relationship with my husband, which is my eternal and consistent preoccupation.) The first is to fulfill all my spiritual obligations as I understand them. The second is to educate my children. Educate in the broadest sense, not just helping them achieve skill and success in school, but giving them a sense of awareness, responsibility, and joy. By far the greatest amount of my time is spent in this endeavor. Third is my responsibility to give the best possible physical care to children and home. If any of these three purposes is neglected, the balance and richness of our family is impaired.

Basic order is essential. This to me means beds, dishes, and general pick-up must be done consistently and directly. Each child makes his bed on rising and clears his own dishes. Clothes washing is done early and late. Hurrah for the men who invented dishwashers, dryers, and permanent press! I am a compulsive picker-upper and throw-awayer; ask any child who has made the mistake of leaving a valuable piece of paper lying around. So the house is mostly neat. Once a week the house is cleaned royally by the entire family. The rest of the time no real cleaning except for accidents or VIP company.

Because the center of the day is too important to be expended on unenduring things, all the routine must be compressed into the early and late hours. Then we can spend the rest of the morning, my little ones and I, reading, doing projects, going to Relief Society, visiting friends, gardening, or singing. The pattern of life is greatly shaped by the houses in which we live.

This California house with its open kitchen and adjoining family room and glass doors is suited to supervising activities with my preschoolers and still working in the kitchen—preparing food, folding clothes, doing dishes, and so forth. My table is piled with papers, crayons, books, and glue. Along one wall are a blackboard and a bulletin board. Teaching is so much a part of my interaction with my children—so many to teach—so much for them to learn. "There are four seasons." "Rains happens this way." "Who is Abraham Lincoln?" "This is how you catch the ball."

I always try to hold at least one church job, not only because it is essential for my own individual spiritual, social, and developmental needs, but also as an example to the children. I love being involved, busy, serving in different ways. My young children often go to the church with me to my meetings. My children feel at home in the church.

At three o'clock the children burst in from school and the house becomes vibrant with them. Imagine how many sheets of school assignments seven children bring home! We are inundated with smudged, gray, blue-lined papers. Practicing, homework, roller-skating, friends, basketball, driving to lessons—and always talking, talking, talking. Ours is a noisy home.

At about seven o'clock my husband arrives home. There is a crescendo of delighted welcome. He is the big event of the day. He makes his way into our bedroom with children clinging to his legs, pockets, and coattails. An audience congregates as he struggles into indestructible home clothes while he is assailed by simultaneous accounts of daily activities, demands for justice, homework problems, and general claims for attention. Those nights when he is gone (traveling, working, or church), the excitement is gone too.

Supper is special because it is the one time we are all together. My recipes are easy and served in stove-to-table cooking pots. I prepare meals with a minimum of utensils and time. The table is set by the children, with a red bowl filled with leaves or flowers and candles in the center. Our nod to gracious living. Evening prayer is held kneeling around the table.

All the children are bathed each night. It is the easiest way to say, "That's the end of the day, my dears!" Our biggest bathroom is awash with clothes, shoes, sand, water, wet towels, and suds. After the little ones are storied to bed, the school children and I gather in a circle on the living-room floor. That is the theory anyway. There is always a feeling of coming and going. We take turns reading from the New Testament and then a short chapter from an older children's book.

Thus begin the long good-nights. Suffice it to say that no one goes to bed without individual encouragement. Gradually the house begins to settle. "I have to finish this page." "I have to give a talk this Sunday." "My report is due tomorrow." "What shall I wear?" "I need another drink." "I forgot my prayer." Another round of kisses. "Good night. We love you." "Go to sleep." "Go to sleep." "Go to sleep."

When my husband is not traveling, we close the day as it began, sharing, laughing, discussing, recreating one another's enthusiasm, love, and joy. One last reassuring look in each room. We love you. We are here.

Precious commitment, eternal vigilance, limitless caring: I think this is the essence of Mormon parenthood. It is the Latter-day Saint concept of eternity that shapes our commitment, sharpens our satisfactions, and enlarges our responsibility. We know the endless nature of parenthood and live with a profound knowledge of the bitter cost if we fail.

Of course, not all days follow this pattern. Weekends are another world, and sometimes the whole system comes to a grinding halt. Illness, an unusual church or community job, a child with a special need, or just an overwhelming day of weariness or frustration can destroy the whole chain. Some days I choose to ignore routine and steal a day for my own use. That is always the day visitors drop in. I wade through the toys, dishes, and children to greet them, knowing that they cannot know all the things I have done that day because what I have not done is so apparent.

It is an irony that motherhood is the one profession that a dedicated and educated adult can practice for a decade and still not be considered an expert. Yet I confess I have confidence in myself and in my role. I believe I do it as well as I am capable of doing anything. I have chosen this life; it does not master me, I master it. I am not its victim, I am its recipient. And if there are times when I wistfully read a university catalogue, or wish that I could run instead of pushing a stroller and observing each leaf and stone, or get tired of the litany of "no's" and "do this's," those times are not frequent and they just serve to confirm that life is a banquet, and, even when filled, we hunger and thirst.

So it is that each day runs its course, filled with being, many things undone, many just begun. And thus to bed . . . and a continuing into the night.

Light from this window:

The time is so brief, we must make it count.

The known is finite, the unknown, infinite. . . .
We stand on an islet in the midst of an
illimitable ocean. . . . Our business in every
generation is to reclaim a little more land.
— Thomas Henry Huxley

Chapter Four

Things I Wish
I'd Known Sooner

When my husband was graduating from Harvard Business School, on the last day of classes General George Doriot, one of his professors, invited students to bring their wives to his final lecture. During the hour and a half in which we sat in the amphitheater of Baker Hall listening to General Doriot, we heard a most astonishing collection of thoughts, advice, wisdom, and personal observations gathered by this remarkable man through a long career of achievement and distinguished business and political connections.

General Doriot did not attempt to connect his advice or give it a pattern. He merely said, "These are some things a successful man should know and do." I remember distinctly his words, delivered in his elegant, French-accented English. "You will take three newspapers wherever you live – the *Wall Street Journal* because you cannot succeed in business without its information; your local newspaper because you must be informed about the community in which you live; and the *New York Times* because it is the most brilliant paper written."

Then he pulled out a copy of the *New York Times* and said, "Now, I will teach you how to read a newspaper so that you will not look undignified, you will not make undo fuss or noise, and you will not get your hands dirty. You must always read the *New York Times* obituary section first because only the lives of significant people are reported there. If you read about how they succeeded, you will be more able to succeed yourselves."

General Doriot then proceeded to show the men and women in the room how to read a newspaper, neatly, crisply, efficiently. For many years when we lived in New York and commuted by train to the city, I was struck with the difference I noted between people who knew how to handle a newspaper well and those who struggled, rattled, and crumpled. General Doriot was right! The ones who knew his "method" looked more composed, and yes, successful.

Many other pieces of advice, as specific and seemingly trivial, were shared: thoughts on dressing, on interviewing, on how to take vacations, on how to eat a business lunch. Each idea was little more than a snippet of advice, and yet each one was applicable to the real lives and challenges these bright, budding executives were soon to face.

Years later perhaps most of those students would be unable to recall the many lessons on business theory and accounting techniques, but most of them would still remember General Doriot's advice on pocket handkerchiefs and what to order at a business lunch (fish — because it is easy to chew and easy to swallow, and thus you can talk more freely).

It has occurred to me that there are many little things I have learned that could have improved the quality of my life had I known them earlier. So perhaps I, like General Doriot, may share some of these scattered bits of knowledge.

I believe it is essential for every woman to recognize that one of her most important roles in life is the creation of homes. This is a cherished gift we can give, both to ourselves and to others. In a lifetime we we will create many homes, beginning with the influence we exert in our childhood homes and the memory and perception of that home that we carry with us into adulthood. We must also create comprehension of our spiritual home, our eternal home, a place of home within our own soul that goes with us wherever we are, in whatever circumstance. We must learn self-esteem and self-motivation so that we are at home with the person we are, and feel comfort and security within that person.

Finally, we need to create our physical home, the four

walls and the roof within which we live and where we have the opportunity to create something wonderful, something intangible, something that gives a sense of welcome, order, love, and vitality, something that becomes a home. Whether we live in a one-room studio, a basement apartment, a small tract home, or a stately home does not matter: the creation of a home within those walls is a demanding challenge. It is a challenge I have faced eighteen times in my marriage.

I have been in great mansions and have felt the cold, hollow echo of rooms where no home existed — only a collection of things. I have been in other magnificent homes where a loving and caring person with generosity and warmth has created the sweetness of a cottage. I have been in small apartments where friends have welcomed me with such graciousness and love that I have felt I was in Kolob — and did not want to leave. From the cluttered, sparsely furnished first homes of young families, to the quiet, memory-filled two-room apartment of an elderly valiant mother — in each place there is a remarkable and unique feeling of home, each created by a remarkable and unique woman.

If we succeed in creating that subtle miracle called a home, what we create will become the rock that gives substance, meaning, and purpose to life. A home is the beginning of the promises of eternity. It will be the thing that will stand, cherished, productive, and valued, long after job changes, mergers, economic cycles, and retirement. Even though the location may change, the four walls come down, the rooms shrink from ten to three, the home that is made within changed confines will remain with the same cherished ingredients still intact as long as we, as women, comprehend our unique stewardship.

Married or single, parent, professional, student— whatever the circumstance of our life, we can create a home that will bless our own life and the lives of others. In ancient England Gothic cathedrals were called the pillars of the earth. The homes we create are the pillars of heaven; they are also the pillars of our mortal society. Winston Churchill said it well when he said, "We create our homes and then our homes create us." What we are, as individuals and as families, is reflected in our homes, measured by our homes, and established in our homes.

Homemaking does not need to be the only thing we do. Many excellent homemakers are productive in far-flung activities and professions, but the priority of home must remain. Without homes where values are learned, emotions are acknowledged, people are cherished, and joyous times are created, our society, as we know it, is lost.

Since this function is undervalued by the world today, women must comprehend, as primary makers of homes, the significance of the task and be self-confirmed in its importance. Inner conviction and knowledge of truth are the great motivators. There may be times when frustrations, loneliness, weariness, other responsibilities, and lack of support will rob the task of its satisfactions and cloud our understanding, but we must never lose our inner conviction of the importance of what we are doing.

I wish I had understood this, clear to the marrow of my bones, much sooner.

Recently while attending some business meetings in

Chicago with my husband, I went to a museum with the wife of a prominent mortgage banker. She is a woman whom I admire and like a great deal. She has character, charm, education, wit, and a wonderful sense of self.

Polly was raised in New England and lived there with her husband for many years. More recently she had moved to the Southwest because of her husband's work. With typical flair, good cheer, and optimism Polly had accepted this upheaval in her life. Almost immediately upon moving she set herself the task of designing and building a home. When it was completed, it was a place of warmth and beauty, a contemporary adaptation of a New England Colonial, with fireplaces, high ceilings, and a spacious entrance hall — everything designed to welcome and embrace, not to impress. She furnished the home with antiques collected by generations of her family, including a mahogany dining room set made by her great-grandfather, a New England cabinetmaker.

The home was as charming, appealing, lovely, and impressive as Polly herself. But the thing that made her home unique was shown in the open house she gave as soon as it was completed. It was a great party, brimming with flowers, food, music, and conversation. Polly invited all of her wide circle of old and new friends — including business associates, neighbors, fellow volunteers from various charity organizations where she worked, members of her book club, grocery store clerks, her doctor and dentist, and many others with whom she came in contact.

Also included in the party were the men who had helped to build the house. These men were the honored guests, from the ditch-diggers to the painters, the carpenters, the men who installed the carpets, the plumbers, and the electricians. She knew them all by name, knew their wives and children, and welcomed them with open arms. As she introduced these people with gratitude and warm affection, Polly commented, "This is really their house, you know. They made it. Without them it wouldn't exist."

Polly has bounteous energy, capability, and creativity. I imagine she could be successful at anything she chose to do.

As we rode to the museum, Polly and I talked about many things. Assuming that a woman with Polly's resources must be involved in some impressive endeavor, I asked, "Well, now that your new home is finished and your youngest son is off to college, what new challenge are you going to take on?" (I know now how many false assumptions are contained in that question.) Polly sat quietly for a moment, then turned to me with a smile and a slight shrug of her shoulders. What she then said pierced me to the quick. It was a moment of insight that I believe every wife and mother should experience with all her heart and spirit, as I did then.

"I just want to keep doing the most important thing, the thing which I love above everything else," she said. "But I want to keep finding ways to do it better. All my life, for the rest of my life, I want to keep being the finest wife, the most loving and caring mother — and, I hope, someday grandmother — it is possible to be. To me, nothing else holds a candle to this in terms of satisfaction and importance. Anything else I do is just my way of saying thank you for the privilege of being a mother."

I was overwhelmed by the strength and depth of the conviction of this sophisticated woman of the world. I thought, "Here I am, a member of a church that has taught me doctrinal truths concerning the eternal nature of these things, and yet I have been so influenced by the pressures of society that I would have been reluctant to give the same answer in this setting. But here is a woman who has spoken these values proudly, knowing them only from the convictions of her own heart."

Thus I was taught something I wish I had known sooner: never to apologize for or waver in the joy and dedication of what I do as a wife and mother, nor to let false voices deter me from a straightforward, inner sense of value and commitment to those roles.

The rest of my list of things I wish I had known sooner are not quite so abstract or noble as this one. They also have very little pattern or organization, since most of them come as unexpectedly as windows of light. I recognize that these are personal learning insights and some of them may be things that apply only to my own life—but they may serve as examples of how we learn from our personal lives, and the varieties of insights that can come through individual experiences.

Lesson One: Have a credit card for identification purposes only. Use it sparingly. Don't even call it a "credit" card; call it an "identification" card. Lives can quickly become enmeshed in indebtedness and bondage when a credit card is used as though it were money. If we do not have the money to pay for an item this month, what makes us believe we will have the money next month—unless we consciously save it up? It is just too easy to flip out the card and buy something we desire. Often the thing we have bought will be used-up or worn-out before the debt is paid.

Lesson Two: Save at least a little money every month. Even a few dollars a month can make a difference. One of the greatest satisfactions in life is to watch a savings account grow. It is somewhat like dieting. At first we love watching the progress; then we hit plateaus when we think we will never reach the next goal. A sudden emergency can deplete the hard-earned total, and the process begins again. However, it is the process that is important. Clark Hinckley, a banker, advises that if we are in debt, we should save rigorously (paying the interest on the debt) until we have saved twice the amount of the debt. Then, as soon as possible, we should pay the debt in full. The reason is that we will still have savings left, and therefore maintain our incentive to save. We need to save for self-discipline, save for security, save for freedom. The amount does not matter. The principle does. At least that is what I have come to believe.

Lesson Three: Try to live within, or even below your means, if possible. A wise woman in a suburb of New York, a person who could have afforded the most expensive home in town, lived in a small, attractive, frugal house, drove a modest car, dressed simply, and was by far the most successful real estate executive in the area. One day she said to me, "You know, Jaroldeen, it is what you keep, not what you make, that makes you wealthy."

Her quiet generosity to countless others, distributed

from her wisely managed wealth, gave her far more personal satisfaction than any showy display of money could possibly have done.

Lesson Four: Learn to manage your money — don't just spend it.

I wish I had learned earlier to do without longer. An empty room is better than one filled with hurriedly bought junk. If I had known earlier what I know now, I would have waited longer and bought better things that would last a lifetime. I wish I had realized that space in a home does not need to be filled. Open rooms are pleasant, especially when the children are small. Undraped rooms and uncarpeted floors can be fresh and bright and very liveable, especially when children are small. One quality piece of furniture is worth several that will be discarded.

Lesson Five: Have at least one good-quality, attractive, conservative outfit to wear whenever it is necessary to meet business or professional groups. Had I known this lesson earlier, it might have saved me many frantic, last-minute, and often unwise purchases. In the early years of my marriage I was careful to see that my husband had a good-quality wardrobe, one appropriate to his work. This was not an extravagance; we felt that it was important if he was to succeed in the business world. I now realize that it is also important for wives to understand that they need to have at least one outfit in which they will feel comfortable in any setting. It is important for self-esteem as well as for practical purposes.

Lesson Six: Make your home, no matter how modest, as lovely as possible. Discover for yourself the gracious touches that are possible and important to you in your own particular circumstances. For the first ten years of our marriage, my husband was a student. Until he obtained his doctorate we lived in truly frugal conditions. We had six children when he received his degree from Harvard, and we had lived in student housing on limited funds for all those years, but my memory of those years is that we lived in comfort and style. This is because I learned to enjoy inexpensive "luxuries." Candles, flowers, ribbons, paper doilies, shiny and clean surfaces, art books and art prints borrowed from the library, beautiful music, soft lights—all of these things give the touch of gracious living in the most simple home and can come within even the most limited budget. Rolls of inexpensive ribbon purchased at a discount house, a spray of parsley in a cup on the kitchen windowsill, jelly beans in a pretty jar, candles on the dinner table, a paper lace doily under a plate of homemade cookies, lemon oil gleaming on scarred wood—all give the feeling of peace, beauty, and plenty.

Lesson Seven: Learn early the principles of order and cleanliness. Details make the difference. Shiny windows and glass doors with fingerprints rubbed off, showers that are scrubbed, floors that shine, a front door that is freshly painted—these are some of the things that make a home look valued and cared-for. We need to focus our efforts. Often we don't need to dust everything; just dusting a table regularly will give the feeling of order. Above all, I have learned and relearned that clutter is the enemy of order and sanity. I wish I had learned earlier to sort, discard, and organize.

Lesson Eight: Buy white linens and white towels. I

learned this after years of making ten beds and cleaning four to five bathrooms a day and sorting tons and tons of laundry. When we visited the Plaza Hotel in New York, I noticed that every piece of linen was white. A window of light. Of course! No sorting. I could use bleach in every load and keep white towels looking like new. No more faded rose, dingy blue, blurred designs, trying to sort darks and lights — in fact, no more sorting at all! All my linens could go in the same load of wash! And nothing is so elegant, or matches every bathroom and bedroom decor so well, as white. No more trying to match the striped sheets, or the Flintstone pillowcases, or the green towels, or giving up in despair and putting the pink flowered top sheet with the navy plaid fitted sheet. It took many years to phase out my old linens, but every time I see a white sale or need to replace old and worn linens, I buy white. This lesson has been a lessening of work and an increase in beauty in my home.

Lesson Nine: Learn to prepare food with aesthetic sense of its beauty, texture, and possibilities. I learned this far too late. For years, without household help, I prepared meals for fifteen people daily. Then I attended a memorable Relief Society homemaking lesson. The long table at the front of the room was covered with a lovely plaid cloth, and on it were displayed beautifully arranged baskets filled with many varieties of apples. The sister who taught the lesson spoke to us of the miracle of apples, described the different varieties, and demonstrated how to prepare several apple dishes. As I watched her hands caress the fruit and create pies, strudels, and dumplings, I suddenly saw the preparation of food in a whole new light. It was an act of artistic creation, a spiritual, tactile, and visual feast. Each apple had become a precious jewel. That vision has not left me.

In summary, I wish I had understood much earlier that home is not a thing to be looked at. It is not something we create to impress others. It is not an object. Home is a living, breathing thing—a laboratory for living. I believe we should each create a home that makes people think, "I want to be *in* that home," not "I wish I *owned* that home."

And finally, I should like to share two things that I learned soon enough, and I have practiced them as well as I could all of my life.

The first of these discoveries is that I have loved raising children. Even the challenges—and there have been many—have given me abiding joy mixed with the sorrow and pain. A friend who had experienced the most tragic event a parent could live through said to me, "Even knowing the end from the beginning, I would not have missed one moment of it." That is how I too feel. I do wish, though, I had known from the first moment of parenting what my father-in-law taught me. "Let 'yes' be your natural response rather than 'no,'" he counseled. I would like to have learned earlier to want to serve more as my children's "facilitator" and less as their "controller."

Last of all, I have known from the moment my life joined my husband's that my greatest joy would come from loving, supporting, and involving myself in his life. The relationship and our functions within it change as the circumstances of our life change, but the priority is constant. We are committed to each other, and we have spent our lives together feeling that we are each involved completely in the cares, concerns, and responsibilities of the other. With patience and interest he has explained his career to me and has allowed me to feel knowledgeable and aware of its many exciting and demanding challenges. In the same way I have woven him into the life of our home, even with his extensive travels and long, long hours of work, so that our children have felt his presence even when he has been away, and he has been completely aware of their concerns and activities.

We are a very normal family. We have done some things well and we struggle to overcome our faults and difficulties, but we are joined together by love, and we each do our part toward achieving our common goals.

What I have learned is perhaps best summarized in an experience we had a few years ago. We were living in Los Angeles, and my husband came home one Saturday after some early meetings and said, "Let's go kite flying."

Off we drove to the Santa Monica beach, about an hour's drive. We sang favorite family songs in the car and laughed and talked. When we arrived at the beach we stared in disbelief at the ocean. There was hardly a wave on the surface. The air was hot and muggy, and, for the first time in our memory, not so much as a breath of air was coming across the water. The children got out their kites and ran, huffing and puffing, along the beach, but the kites simply dragged in the sand. They turned to their father with disappointment in their faces as listless as the kites.

"There has to be wind somewhere in Los Angeles," Weston said with conviction and enthusiasm. "Get back in the car and we'll find it." So all fourteen of us piled back in.

Through the long afternoon we drove through the streets of Los Angeles, stopping at parks and open lots. No wind. But we never lost heart. Father was driving, and I poured my energy into the time we spent in the car, telling stories, pointing out the sights, laughing, talking, singing. At last, late in the afternoon, we arrived at Griffith Park.

"There it is," my husband said, pointing upward, "the highest point in the city. There must be some wind up there!"

And so we climbed up the highest hill in the park. There, perched on the very roof of the city, overlooking the park, the planetarium, and the great stretches of streets, houses, and skyscrapers, we clung to the narrow summit of a treeless mountain and felt the gentle updraft of warm air. My husband took the ball of string and played one of the kites into the air. The soft breeze caught the bright wings of the kite and carried it upward, and we all stood together on the crowded hilltop, holding one another and smiling upward as our kite flew bravely into the sun.

Light from this window:

When we know what we are searching for, and if we refuse to give up, there will be many times when we will be privileged to find the lift of the rising air, and oh, how our kites will soar!

The seed however broadcast will catch
somewhere and produce its hundredfold.
— Theodore Parker

Chapter Five

Wildflower Seeds

For many years we lived in Connecticut in a wonderful
house that looked like a converted barn, with lawn in the
front and a backyard of natural woods. Brambles of wild
blackberries and rhododendron bushes were hidden in
the tangled growth, while volunteer wisteria vine trailed
the front of our fence. Old, moth-eaten dogwood trees
lined the road and the stone fence that fronted the
property.

We loved that house, the village, our neighbors, and
the glorious display of nature as each season tried to outdo
the others. It was impossible to choose a favorite time of
year. Spring, with daffodils blanketing the clear fields and

rimming the houses, the fresh green fuzz on the dark branches of the trees that arched the narrow, winding roads, and the balmy ocean-scented breezes coming across Long Island Sound. Summer, with its deeply shaded woodlands, the sun filtering through the rustling leaves, the lush lawns and exuberant growth of vine, bush, and flower, and the hot, lazy afternoons. Autumn, unrestrained, lavish, a kaleidoscope of colors too brilliant and vibrant for the eye to hold, prodigal in harvest and in beauty. Winter, with the gentle silence of falling snow, blue, silver, and white, winds that chased us indoors to the sweet warmth of a crackling fire. Who could choose a favorite season from these bounties?

In such surroundings the symbiotic relationship of man and nature becomes very natural, and, as a result, I spent a great deal of time in the local nursery and garden shop, looking for something to grow, either indoors or outdoors, depending on the season. It was there that I bought my first flower bulbs, and I watched with maternal joy as the tulips, daffodils, and jonquils sprang from the earth the following spring. It was there that I learned that zucchini will grow when nothing else in the world will.

It was there that I discovered, for my indoor, winter plants, the wonders of Aspergris fern, Reiger begonias, cyclamen, grape hyacinth, and paper-white narcissus for Christmas, and a massive wreath of dried bay-leaves for my kitchen. I loved that garden shop!

One spring day I was browsing while the clerk wrote up my order for some bedding plants. I noticed on a table that featured a number of sale items a dusty plastic bag full of something that looked like grass seed. The bag was not large, about the size of a pound of confectioner's sugar, and it had no commercial label, only a piece of paper glued to the plastic. The label read "Wildflower Seeds." And under that title was this explanation: "These seeds are indigenous to this part of Connecticut. If you broadcast these seeds in a meadow, swampy area, or wooded grove, flowers will grow. The flowers which grow will vary according to the season; sunlight, soil, and moisture conditions of the place they are planted. Only those flowers will grow which flourish in those specific conditions. The other seeds will remain dormant. However, it is guaranteed that wherever you broadcast these seeds, some flowers will grow."

I was absolutely intrigued. In my imagination I had already broadcast the seeds across the lower reaches of our front lawn, and I could see the results — flowers dancing in the sun, in all shades and varieties. I could imagine charming bouquets of wildflowers on my dining room table, such a wonderful conversation piece, and another part of nature brought into the circle of our everyday experience.

I glanced once again at the dusty little bag. The price tag was old and blurred, but it was decipherable. "One-ninety-eight." How wonderful! A dollar and ninety-eight cents. Not much to pay for an experiment that could be so rewarding. I placed the bag next to my other purchases. "I'll take this too, Jim," I said to the clerk.

He glanced up at me with a surprised look. "Are you sure, Mrs. Edwards?" he asked.

"Well, I know it's a bit of a gamble, and probably none

of the flowers will grow," I answered, "but I figure it's still worth a dollar ninety-eight."

"Look again," Jim said, pointing at the label.

I looked again, and this time I saw more clearly.

"A hundred and ninety-eight dollars!" I gasped. "For this little bag? Why on earth would it be so expensive?"

Jim smiled. "It isn't easy to gather wildflower seeds," he said. "They are very rare and precious."

As I drove home without the wildflower seeds, I contemplated how much women are like wildflowers. To our Heavenly Father we are each rare and precious. When we are born our nature is sown with dormant seeds. Talents, wisdoms, questions, characteristics, dreams, capabilities—all broadcast within us as silent, fragrant possibilities. Each condition and season of our lives causes different seeds to sprout within us. And many still continue to lie dormant, just waiting for the right conditions to bloom with unexpected beauty.

Who knows what will bloom within us during the open, sunny-meadow days of our lives? What quiet seeds lie waiting for the dark, shadowed, wooded days? Or what generous and hardy plant will suddenly sprout when our life turns into a treacherous swamp? Perhaps the darkest moment is when the most glorious flowers burst into blossom.

We once moved into a home in California with a garden planted with unfamiliar tropical flora. Late one night, having spent a long day doing laundry, tending a sick child, and trying to unpack boxes, I turned off the last light and prepared to go upstairs to bed. Before locking the front door, I opened it for a moment to take a deep breath of the cool night air. The moon was silver on the trees, but the night had a warm, dark feeling. I breathed deeply, and a sweet fragrance filled my lungs. The night seemed to sing with perfume, and I looked about me in wonder.

Next to the door, a plant that had hitherto escaped my notice, a rather straggly bush, had shot forth a tall, white stalk covered with blossoms. During the day the stalk had looked like a green knobby spike that needed to be pruned. But here, in the night, its green buds had opened and the white flowers were filling the blackness with a fragrance so sweet it was like a balm. The plant was night-blooming ginger, which flowers only in the darkest hours. During the day it would merit scarcely a glance.

It is this unexpectedness in ourselves and in our lives that makes the revelations of mortality so precious. The discovery of truth and knowledge, the discovery of the possibilities within us, requires that we be tested in every season, in every clime, in every condition. It is the only way that the dormant seeds within us will have the opportunity to flower.

Light from this window:

We are like gardens sown with endless possibilities. We should not fear the changing seasons.

Be our joys three parts pain!
Strive, and hold cheap the strain;
Learn, nor account the pang; dare,
    never grudge the throw!
                          — Robert Browning

Chapter Six

Three Lessons from Pain

My favorite novel is *My Lady of Cleves* by Margaret Campbell Barnes. In the final scene of the novel, Anne of Cleves is comforting Henry the Eighth as he lies dying. She realizes that this monarch, who has been the most powerful man on the earth, is afraid to die.

"Henry," she says softly, "it has been my experience that the things we fear the most are often the things which come to happen. I have found that if we turn to meet them, and walk toward them with our head held high, we can walk right through them. And we are always better on the other side."

Never has a mother feared streets more than I did. My children were not allowed to cross streets by themselves until they were old enough to drive! Even then, I still preferred to hold my teenagers' hands and tell them, "Look both ways." My idea of an ideal world was one in which children and cars *never* had to be on the same thoroughfare—sort of like a big block with everything on it, so no one ever had to cross the street.

I suspect it was inevitable, then, that *I* would be the one who would get hit by a car.

On a bright, sunny, summer morning, out for a healthy walk, I crossed my street on a green light just as a young man in a big car decided to make a righthand turn on his red light. I had seen his car stopped at the intersection and was sure he had seen me, but as I stepped off the curb, to my astonishment I saw the glint of something moving. I glanced back over my left shoulder. It was the hood ornament—and it was coming toward me!

In the next instant the bumper hit my knee and I felt my leg explode beneath me. I fell under the car like a stone and lay there, pinned, as the turning wheel moved straight toward my head. By now I was fully aware that the driver had not seen me and was still unaware that I was under his car. A terrible death seemed certain. But then I heard his passenger scream at him to stop, and even though he did not know why, he stopped. I am so thankful for those seconds in which my life was surely spared.

As the ambulance carried me to the hospital, I began

what would be months of operations, complications, disability, confinement, and profound pain. There were many nights when, in the lonely darkness of my room, I wept to be spared the agony—to be able to find some relief. I watched precious time slip through my helpless fingers. I despaired of ever walking again. I chafed at my weakness and longed to be myself again.

Only slowly did I come to an acceptance of what I had been taught since childhood: that adversity brings strength, sorrow brings joy, and pain brings us the most priceless gifts. The value of something is often the equal of its price, so it is logical that the gifts of pain are infinitely precious—they are so dearly bought.

John Donne declared that we should never try to take another's tribulations from them. We would just as well rob the gold from their pockets.

I would like to share with you three of the lessons that pain has taught me in these past months.

The first lesson is perhaps the most valuable in a practical sense. It is the lesson I learned from the wisdom of a dear friend, an immensely busy person, who had taken the time to come and sit beside me. From the depths of my pain, in that precious quiet moment of friendship I felt free to ask her a difficult question, something that had puzzled me during the years I had known her.

"Ruth," I said (this is not her real name), "I'm not handling this experience very well. My feelings and attitudes are all wrong. May I ask you a very personal question? Since we have been friends I have watched you go through many of the worst experiences it is possible to experience—grave financial reverses, a dramatic change of life-style, challenges with your children, a death in your family. Through it all, you never change. You're always gentle, kind, generous with your home and your possessions, loving toward all whom you know, and faithful in your church callings. I *know* these things affect you deeply, yet you never show fear, anger, bitterness, disappointment, or gloom. I must know how you meet life with such steadfast faith and good cheer."

She looked at me for a long moment as she thought, and then she gave me a beautiful smile. "Jaroldeen," she answered, "whenever something difficult happens to me, I never question what has happened. I never ask, '*Why* did this have to happen to me?' or '*Why* must I go through this?' or '*Why* would the Lord let this happen?' or '*Why* won't this go away?' or '*Why* aren't my prayers being answered?'

"I don't let myself worry about what can't be changed. All I worry about is 'What is my role?' and 'How does the Lord want me to act?' and 'What does the Lord want me to do?' and 'What goals must I set to change this?' and 'What must I do to turn this into a building experience for me and my family?' "

As I listened to her, I realized that not one of the questions she asked began with *why*. She understood that any growth that comes from pain and challenge can come only after we have stopped asking why. Growth begins when we have accepted what now *is* and what is *past*. Asking questions of ourselves and the Lord that begin with *why* is like racing the motor of our car without putting it in gear.

My son returned from his mission many weeks after

my accident. I was still very weak, restricted in my activities, and unable to walk. As we drove past the intersection where the accident had occurred, I said, rather dramatically, "On that very spot! On June 21, my life was changed."

"Don't do that, Mother," my son said gently.

"What?" I asked, surprised.

"Don't make an occasion out of it. Don't remember it that way. It gives it too much power over you."

He was right. The first thing we must do in order to begin to gain the lessons from pain is to accept what is past and let it go. Then we must begin to ask ourselves the *what* questions: What am I still able to do? What is the Lord teaching me? What goals should I set?

The wonder of asking questions that begin with "What" is that it puts our life back in our own hands, with the Lord guiding us. We are no longer the victim of circumstances—we are now in control of our future. We have taken the reins of our free agency back in our own hands. Fear, anger, resentment, bitterness, confusion, and frustration only steal free agency from us.

The second great gift from pain is *love.*

Pain is the catalyst that breaks the heart open and teaches the spirit to be contrite. As one's heart is opened, it can be taught the immensity of love.

When do we feel the greatest love for the Savior? Of course we love and adore him as we think of his glorious birth. We praise and love him as we think of his baptism, of his obedience, of his striding across the hills of Galilee, performing miracles, and feeding the five thousand. We love and feel anguish for him in the last week of his ministry as he once again teaches in Jerusalem. For many, our love for him almost overwhelms us when we contemplate him in the Garden of Gethsemane. As we think of the time of his bitterest pain, when he bore our sins and griefs, our hearts burn with love.

It was such love, born of pain, that gave Orson Whitney a vision of the Savior in the Garden. At the end of the vision, Elder Whitney was privileged to see the Lord preparing to return to His Father. So great was Elder Whitney's love at that moment that he threw himself at the Savior's feet and begged to go with him. The Savior looked into his eyes with such love, understanding, and compassion that to read of it makes us weep.

Joseph Smith, in Liberty jail, also caught a glimpse of the Savior's plan and of his boundless love. When Joseph cried out in agony, "O Lord, how long shall they [the Saints] suffer," the Lord spoke to him and reminded him that he, the Son of God, had "descended below them all." He then reassured the Prophet, "All these things shall give thee experience, and shall be for thy good." (D&C 121:3; 122:8, 7.)

It is when our hearts are full of sorrow that we are able to borrow the "balm of Gilead," which balm is a deepened understanding of our Savior's love for us.

Through trial, we may gain greater love for our family and a greater appreciation of their love for us. Even after all the years of serving my husband and my children and loving them as deeply as I thought it was possible for anyone to love, I have found that through the process of being served by them, I have gained a sweet and tender enlargement of my emotions that I had not dreamed before.

Pain requires that we let those who love us serve us. In times of dependence, beautiful things occur.

On the night of my bone-grafting operation, my three daughters came to my hospital room. Because of my re-action to the medication, the room was kept bitterly cold. It was a very small, dreary private room, crammed with machines, tubes, bottles, and monitors. Heavily sedated, I could barely make out the faces of my daughters, two of them teenagers and the other a newly called missionary. They had each brought a light blanket or quilt, and all through the long night and the next day they remained with me, talking quietly, coming to my bedside at the slightest sound, sweetly encouraging me, and carrying on conversation even though I could not speak. Although my eyes were closed I was acutely aware of their presence. It was immeasurably reassuring to me, more beautiful than I can say. I shall never forget it.

Weeks later I was still unable to reach my feet. They were rough and dry, and I could not care for them. Al-though it was one of the most humbling things I have ever done, I asked my husband if he would care for my feet. He looked at me with tears in his eyes and said, "Thank you." As he cared for my feet I understood the meaning of the ordinance of the washing of feet. I have never felt so loved, or loved so much in return.

Only through pain, and the humility that comes from adversity, can such cherished and unspeakably dear mo-ments pierce our hearts. We would not choose to have such experiences, but we would not part with the gifts of such moments at any price.

Through suffering, we gain an increased awareness of love for all mankind. It illuminates our hearts and minds and gives us a burning desire to help, lift, and protect. Once harmed or hurt, we gain a great desire to care for others who are in need or pain.

The third gift of pain is recognition of the need to cherish each moment. *Right now* is the best we have — it is all we have.

A friend called from Arizona to see how I was doing. She had just attended a women's conference and was a little discouraged. "You know," she said, "the young mothers were just not happy about their lives. They seemed to feel trapped and unappreciated and unchallenged. One of them said, 'I get so tired of trying to fix supper with one child clinging to my leg, another on my hip, and the third one crying to be picked up.' "

I understand how that young woman felt, but a great sense of sadness came over me. Have we so failed today's generation of mothers that they see the years of bearing and rearing children as punishment rather than privilege?

For just a few years in a whole lifetime, there is that brief window to tenderly raise — and enjoy — the individuals who will be the most important to us throughout eternity. Yet how many women spend those years resenting the limitations, wishing the children were grown up and away from home?

The important principle of life is that each moment, each season carries within it its own special rewards, joys, and efforts. The greater the efforts, the greater the rewards. The secret is to see each moment for what it has to yield and then grasp it.

For example, during the child-rearing years, what do we complain about? Chauffeuring. "Oh," we say, "all I do is drive the children places. This year I have to drive Johnny *every day* from kindergarten. I feel like I'm in prison!"

In reality, what is driving but the best opportunity to get a child's news "hot off the griddle"? For nine months we have the splendid chance to sit next to someone we love with all our heart — away from the phone and other chores — and *listen*.

One day, as I was driving my son home from kindergarten, he looked up at me and said, "I've got to do homework today."

"What homework?" I asked.

"We have to do an oral report on an animal. We have to tell three facts about it. I've chosen polar bears."

"Wonderful!" I replied, eager to teach him research skills. "We'll go right home and get out the encyclopedia."

This was beginning to sound like work to William. "I don't need the encyclopedia," he said firmly. "I already have my facts. Remember when we went to the San Diego zoo? They told me all about polar bears and I remember."

I decided to call his bluff.

"All right," I said. "What are your three facts?"

He began confidently. "Do you know why polar bears are white?"

"Why?"

"So they can blend in with the snow and their predators won't see them."

"Good," I said. "What's the next fact?"

"Do you know that polar bears have fur on the bottoms of their feet so they won't stick to the ice?"

This was a fact I hadn't known so I applauded. "Good fact! And what's the third one?"

From the look on his face I could tell he didn't have a third one, but the specter of being chained to an afternoon with the encyclopedia spurred him on.

"Well," he said, after a little pause. "Do you know why polar bears have blue eyes?"

This was a fact I was sure I had never heard. "No," I said. "Why?"

"So that," William said slowly and carefully, "when they dive into the water, they can open their eyes and it camouflages them in the blue water, and the seals can't see them and they can catch them." His smile was triumphant.

I looked him in the eye and shook my head, and we both started to laugh. To this day I love the image of blue-eyed polar bears swimming around in the ocean with eyes open so no one can see them. Who would miss such a moment!

If we wish away the moments, they will be gone. The things we have wanted to leave — the mess, the noise, the obligations — will be gone, but so will the children! This is true of every moment of life. If we do not see its joys, if we do not make the most of it, it will pass — and so will its opportunities.

I remember a day, when I was a young girl, when my father came home early in the afternoon. It must have been a Saturday, because my brothers and I were home from school. Mother was at the sink, doing the dishes, and wearing a pretty apron with a big bow in the back.

Father came in and said, "Come on, let's drive up to Livingston and I'll show you the new ranch."

He had just bought a new ranch and none of us had seen it. It was about eighty miles away, up in the foothills of the Canadian Rockies.

"No, Charles," Mother said. "There's too much work to be done. I haven't finished the dishes and the children haven't done their chores. We have to shop and get ready for tomorrow. We just can't go."

Father went over to Mother, untied her apron, and, with a little laugh, twirled her around. Then he kissed her and said, "The dishes will wait."

We couldn't believe that Mother agreed! But off we went. We didn't even have time to change our clothes. We picked up cold cuts, bread, and fruit at a little general store in one of the small towns we drove through after we left the city, and by midafternoon we arrived at the ranch property. We had not seen any signs of habitation for miles, only the great mountains coming closer, and the lush green foothills, and the dusty road winding between the long barbed-wire fences.

"This is where our property starts," Father said, waving his hand. "I think there's a stream beyond that little hill. Why don't we go down there to have our lunch?"

We grabbed the grocery bags and a blanket, squeezed through the barbed wire, and started up the hill. At the crest we stopped in astonishment. The whole slope of the field as it fell away toward the sparkling stream was a blanket of wild tiger lilies, as crimson as a king's velvet robe. It was like coming across the poppy field in *The Wizard of Oz*. Such unexpected glory! Such treasured memories! A parent will never say with regret, "I wish I hadn't done so much with my children," or "I wish I hadn't spent so much time caring for my family," or "I wish we hadn't had so much fun together," or "I wish I hadn't loved them so much."

It is through prayer that the blessings of pain can be perceived and realized. Many times I have wept and the words of the children's song have come unbidden to my mind: "Heavenly Father, are you really there? And do you hear and answer every child's prayer?" This song was sung by my grandchildren, and when they sang it, their mother sang in response in her loving voice, "Pray, he is there. Speak, he is listening." As I wept, I heard my daughter's voice in song, and her testimony lifted my faith, and I could pray.

And so, I try to turn and face the hard things, to walk toward them with my head held high. I wish to remember the three lessons I have learned: (1) Accept what has happened and concern myself only with what the Lord wishes me to do now. (2) Let my heart rejoice in the renewed awareness of being loved and of loving my Savior, my family, and my fellowmen. (3) Discover and enrich each glorious moment.

Light from this window:

The lessons of pain are dearly learned but are doubly sweet.

I feel very strongly about putting questions;
You start a question and it is like starting a stone.
You sit quietly on the top of a hill;
And away the stone goes.
— Robert Louis Stevenson

Chapter Seven

My First "What" Question

My tenth child was almost born on an airplane somewhere between New York and California. Weston had
taken a new position in Los Angeles, and the plan was
simple. He would drive the nine children across the country and get into our new house, while I remained behind
in the East, had the baby, and then flew to join the family
within two to three weeks.

Great plan. The only problem was, the baby had other
ideas. Three weeks went by, the children were safely in

Los Angeles, the furniture had arrived, but not the baby. I remained in New Jersey.

Finally Weston had to report to work, so our two oldest daughters, young teenagers, were having to manage the family. Every night I would call. "What are you eating?" I'd ask.

"Oh, soup and junk," was the answer. (The soup sounded okay, but the "junk" was a concern.)

"Why only soup?" I asked.

"The stove isn't working," was the response. "We have to use a hot plate."

"We don't *have* a hot plate," I objected.

"We borrowed one from the neighbors," the children replied cheerfully.

"What are you doing about keeping your clothes clean?" I asked.

"No problem," they answered blithely. "We just swim in our shorts and T-shirts and then the sun dries them."

At this point I had an image of my poor, motherless children in wet clothes, barefoot, walking from door to door, begging for hot plates. I immediately decided that I would never be able to face our new neighbors. When and if I ever got to Los Angeles, we would just have to move!

The next day I went to my obstetrician and begged him to write a note to get me aboard an airplane. He could see how desperate I was and so he said, "I think it would be all right. After all, you'll be in Los Angeles in five hours. What can happen in five hours?"

He was an obstetrician, and he knew perfectly well what could happen in five hours.

No sooner had the plane taken off than I thought to myself, "It's nothing but indigestion." A few minutes later I muttered, "Nerves. It's just nerves." Another few minutes later, however, I had to acknowledge what it really was. I was in labor!

I wish I could tell you that my only concern was for the baby. And, in all honesty, I was very concerned for the baby—but my greatest concern at that moment was the fact that I felt I was about to be the star in a real-life documentary. I was seriously asking myself if it might be possible to have a baby on an airplane and not have anybody notice. However, giving up that line of thinking as futile, I stopped a passing flight attendant and whispered to her, "I'm having a baby." She looked at me with an impatient sigh and a look that said, "That's rather obvious."

"No," I whispered. "I mean, I think I'm having the baby right now."

I'll give her credit that she didn't drop her tray, but she did lose her smile. She roared up the aisle, grabbed the microphone, and shouted, "Is there a doctor on board?"

Everyone on the plane stood up and stared at me, then began whispering. So much for anonymity. As it turned out, there was a doctor aboard the plane. She was sitting right next to me.

I was moved into first class with the doctor, and she sat and timed my pains as the plane continued to wing across the continent. We talked quietly, and the pains continued but did not get worse.

At last the captain announced that we were approaching the Los Angeles airport. We both heaved a sigh of relief. At about the same time, the pains stopped. "Probably the pressurized cabin," the doctor said.

I prepared to deplane but was told to keep my seat until the plane was empty. The passengers filing by gave me very disappointed looks, as though they had been reading a book and hadn't been able to read the last chapter.

After the passengers had left the plane, four men in white leaped on board. Before I knew what was happening, they had me strapped to a hospital gurney and were wheeling me through the terminal building.

I protested that I was fine, and begged to join my husband and family, but they wouldn't listen or stop. You can imagine what a ten-month pregnant woman lying flat on her back on a gurney cart looks like!

One of my children caught sight of me as I sped past, and she cried, "Mother, where are you going?" Then all nine children started racing after the gurney. Weston turned and joined the running procession in his three-piece suit, carrying his briefcase—but he was also trying to look like he didn't know who any of these people were!

As I was whisked into an ambulance I called to him, "Find out where they're taking me, and come and get me." The next thing I knew, I was speeding through the heart of Los Angeles, explaining to the medics that I was no longer in labor, and watching palm trees whip by the windows.

At the hospital the admitting clerk was very impatient. "Who is your doctor?" she asked.

I tried to explain that I had just arrived in town and had no doctor.

She stared at me, disbelieving, and angrily repeated, "Who is your doctor?"

"I am planning to call an old friend who practices obstetrics somewhere in the metropolitan area," I said. "But I have no idea what suburb he practices in. I was going to look him up."

"What's his name?" she snapped.

"Keith Merrill," I snapped back, having lost patience by now. "I'll call him as soon as you let me out of here."

Without a word she wheeled me into a small examination room, closed the door, and left me.

By now I was thoroughly frustrated. "Please, Weston," I whispered to myself. "Find me, and spring me!"

Just then I heard a voice over the hospital intercom: "Dr. Keith Merrill. Dr. Keith Merrill."

That did it. Hadn't anyone listened to me? I *told* that woman I had no idea where he practiced. Why on earth were they paging him?

Just then the door opened and Dr. Keith Merrill walked in with a nurse. "I don't have a patient named Mrs. Edwards," he was saying in an exasperated voice, and then he stopped and stared at me lying on the table.

We had not seen each other for more than fifteen years, not since high school. "Jaroldeen!" he exclaimed. "Jaroldeen Edwards! What are you doing here . . . and in *that* condition?"

I knew I had just been asked one of life's great questions. It took me nearly two days of pondering to come up with the true and satisfying answer. "Creating," is what I should have replied. "Creating a new life. Creating a new home. Creating a wiser and better 'me.'" At that particular phase of my life, at that time of frustration and uncertainty, hard work and upheaval, discovering the answer to Keith's seminal question gave me great peace of mind. Everything fell into a meaningful direction.

Since that day I have thought of Keith's question many times. I have found that if I can answer it to my own satisfaction — and to the satisfaction of the Lord — I feel a sense of well-being. When I start to lose my grip on who and what I am, when life begins to lose its edge or fades into something close to chaos or anarchy, I ask myself Keith's question. What am I doing here? and what is my condition? The answer, when I am able to think through to it, reimbues my life with a sense of purpose and worth.

Sometimes, when my life is off course, the answer brings me up short. I find that I am where I am for the wrong reasons, or with the wrong attitude, or I have wandered away from my real purposes. The answer to the question sometimes enables me to walk away from wrong choices when I ask, "What am I doing here?" and the answer reveals a lost sense of direction.

My daughter experienced the strength of this question when she pledged for a social club her freshman year at a university. One evening, in the midst of pledge activities, she overheard a remark made by a member of the club's pledge committee. "She's pretty enough and rich enough to be a good member," the young woman said, speaking of one of the potential candidates.

Suddenly my daughter asked herself, "What am I doing here?" She looked down at the items of clothing the pledges had been required to wear. "And in this condition?"

73

The answer was clear to her. She was sitting in a place where values that mattered to her and goals that she felt were important were not well served. "I'm in the wrong place," she concluded. She simply stood up and walked out. "I don't think I'm a good candidate for membership," she later told us with a smile.

On the other hand, the answer to Keith's question can sometimes be enormously satisfying, ratifying, and give meaning to the most unexpected events.

One day I sat on a small kindergarten-size chair, with my knees up to my chin, listening to the rhythm band of my twelfth child's preschool group. It was really a dreadful concert, slow and out of tune. I had a dozen important things to do, and this little concert was not an important event, sort of a "come if you like" activity—a practice, actually. Only a handful of other mothers had bothered to come. I rubbed my aching back and thought that I could not even count the number of such concerts I had attended through the years. Who would remember? Not me, and probably not my children. Surely now, in my mature years, it wasn't necessary to attend everything.

As I squirmed impatiently in the little chair, I heard Keith's question pop unbidden into my mind. *What am I doing here?*

Just then my little daughter looked over at me and smiled. My answer to the question came, as solid and satisfying as the rock on which the wise man placed his house. *I'm building a child.* Suddenly the chair became comfortable and the concert seemed rare, precious, and fleeting.

Nothing in my life has been very predictable. I am

consistently astonished when I pause to think about it. The places I have lived, the people I have known, the problems that have arisen, the opportunities that have opened, and the possibilities that have remained closed — all of these things are a source of amazement to me. But if I am in my spot, for the right purposes, and in the right condition, all is well.

Light from this window:

The right questions form the bedrock for the right answers.

Love is enough,
though the world be a-waning.
—William Morris

Chapter Eight

Niagara Falls

After seven years of marriage and five children, my husband finished his doctoral degree and we headed for the "real world," (The "real world," in our case, was Chicago and a job with an investment firm.)

In the years of our marriage we had lived on Wright-Patterson Air Force Base in Ohio and then in Harvard student housing—always in apartments. In the last months before Weston's degree was completed, I discovered we were expecting our sixth child, and I began to be impatient. I wanted to live in a real home. The weeks seemed to drag as he finished his dissertation, and when, at last, his doctoral committee heard his final arguments and the dissertation was accepted, I rejoiced — not only because of Weston's wonderful achievement, but also because it signaled my opportunity to finally have a home in which to live.

Weston was flown to Chicago, where he accepted a wonderful job offer. He also rented a large, old home in Wilmette. Then he flew back to Cambridge to gather us up in our old Chevrolet to make the trip to Illinois.

It was the dead of winter. The skies were gray and leaden, the roads treacherous, and our little car over-crowded. Our youngest child, who was then seven months old, was very irritable. She was recovering from an ear infection and had to be given medicine every four hours. She hated the taste of the bright pink liquid and persisted in spitting it up, so that everything in the front seat seemed to be spotted with the sticky, pink stuff.

I know now that adding to the stress of the trip was my own mental attitude. I felt, deep inside, that I had waited longer than was reasonable to have a home of my own. The long wait had caused in me an intense yearning, a feeling of entitlement, almost an obsession, to get settled, to have space, stability, and the chance to create a sub-stantial nest. Perhaps the best way to say it would be that I was *home*-sick, that is, I was sick with the desire to be in my own home.

As the miles passed I became increasingly anxious to have the trip over. I wanted desperately to be someplace where I could begin to make a home. If I did not feel resentment, I certainly felt justified impatience.

When we neared Niagara Falls, Weston said, "I know it's winter, but I still think we should stop and let the children see the falls. They may never have another chance."

"No, please," I said. "Let's just keep going. The sooner we get to Wilmette the better. I just want to get settled!"

"Dear," Weston said reasonably, "let's try to make this trip a bit of a vacation for the children. We won't have another break for a long time."

Late in the afternoon we turned off the highway and drove through the deserted streets of Niagara Falls and out onto Goat Island. Except for the parking-lot attendant, we were the only people on the island. Weston parked near the entrance, where the lone attendant huddled in his heated booth.

The baby was crying. We were out of milk. The sun was beginning to go down. But, with his infectious enthusiasm, Weston ran with the children across the empty parking lot to the viewing platform. There, in the bitter cold wind, they looked down on the ice-rimmed glory of the falls.

Soon they came running back toward the car, laughing and excited, their cheeks rosy with the cold. Weston insisted that I must go and look at the falls. He took the crying baby, and, with great reluctance, I climbed out of the car and went over to look.

The sight was glorious, but as I came back, I looked at our car. Something didn't seem right. The luggage rack looked like a crazy hat tilted on top. Then I realized. The rear tire was as flat as an airless balloon!

By now the three youngest children were crying. When he opened the trunk, Weston discovered that our spare tire was also flat. We caught the parking attendant just as he was preparing to leave, and he put in a call to a garage. Then he left for home. We sat, alone, in the vast parking lot, staring at the thundering falls as the sun set and night gathered in the surrounding trees.

It was almost an hour before we saw the flickering lights of a wrecker coming toward us. We were towed off the island and taken to a garage, where quick repairs were made. Then we hunted for a motel. The city of Niagara Falls is like a ghost town in the winter, with most motels closed, but we finally found a small establishment that had a vacant two-bedroom unit with two cribs. Obviously the motel was not expecting guests, for the room was dusty and cold. We did get the heat working, and Weston ran down the street to a diner and brought back hot soup, crackers, and milk. After feeding the children, I prepared to give them baths.

We had seen a drugstore a block away, and Weston said he would go down to it and get some more medicine for the baby. I was busy running water into the tub, so I called my thanks to him over my shoulder.

After I bathed the five children, I zippered them into their fluffy pajama suits. I tucked the older ones in bed and put the two youngest in the cribs. One of the cribs was broken, and I spent some time figuring how to prop it up on some chairs.

The children were excited and restless so we talked, and I sang songs with them, and finally I told them a story. I turned off all the lights in the room, leaving just a tiny glow from the adjoining room, and lay down on the bed with them. One by one they finally fell asleep.

As the room became quiet, I began to feel uneasy.

Where was Weston? I didn't have a watch with me, but it seemed to me it had been well over an hour since he had left, and the drugstore was less than a block away.

I took a bath and prepared for bed. At any moment I expected him to walk in, but time moved slowly, endlessly, and he did not come. Finally I got up and got dressed again. I sat by the window and watched the road. There was very little traffic, and as a set of headlights would start down the block my hopes would rise, only to be dashed when the vehicle moved on. The motel was in a rundown section of the city, and the streets looked dreary, deserted, and mean.

There was no phone in our rooms and I was terrified to leave the children alone, but by now I was certain that Weston had been gone for over three hours, and I knew the drugstore was closed. I could think of no explanation for his absence. Fear had grown in me that something dreadful had happened to him. Maybe he had been mugged or had been in an automobile accident.

Finally I left the room, locked it, and went to the manager's office to ask if I could use his phone. He had been sleeping and was very curt. "No," he said. "Guests are required to use the pay phone at the corner."

Since the pay booth was in view of our doorway, I ran to use the phone. It was bitterly cold and my voice was shaking with chill and fear. I found the number for the police department in the phone book and dialed. "Officer," I said, when a voice answered. "Could you please tell me if there have been any automobile accidents or crimes reported in the last three hours. My husband left our motel room over three hours ago to do a brief errand and he hasn't returned. I'm afraid something might have happened."

"Lady," said a bored voice, "does your husband drink?"

"No," I cried. "No. He is the most wonderful, responsible, caring man in the world."

"Well, there haven't been any auto accidents. That's all I can tell you."

As I walked back toward the room, I felt a heavy cloak of fear and worry, but piercing the weight of my fear was a sudden overwhelming realization of how precious my husband was to me. It was as though my heart was filled to bursting with the power of my love for him, my gratitude and joy for his strength and goodness, and the immensity of my need for him. I understood, perhaps for the first time, that everything good, sweet, and secure in my life came from and through him. Standing there in the dark, I had never felt my love for him more strongly — and I had also never felt more bereft and alone.

Just then a pair of headlights shone through the window, and I turned to see our car pulling into the motel. Weston climbed wearily out of the driver's seat.

"Where have you been?" I asked, tears streaming down my face as I opened the door.

With tenderness he held me close. "Didn't you hear me?" he asked, astonished. "I called to you as I was leaving. I went back to the garage to pick up the other tire, and they hadn't even started working on it. I've never seen slower mechanics, but we couldn't leave tomorrow without a working spare."

I couldn't even answer him, I was crying so hard from relief and exhaustion.

"I'm so sorry," he said. "I couldn't phone you, because there's no phone in the room. I just thought you'd know I'd run into a snag at the garage."

"I didn't hear you — the water was running," I managed to gulp. "I thought you were just going down the street for m-m-medicine."

We didn't say any more. More tired than we knew, we lay down on the bed, and I cried until the warmth of his arms and the quiet of the room calmed my heart. Weston fell asleep, but I lay there beside him in that wretched, dusty room, in that alien city, with the lumpy beds, the broken crib, and the unknown world surrounding us, and I knew something that I have never forgotten. I was home.

Light from this window:

We don't need walls, or rooms, or gardens, or furniture, or flowers, or familiar scenes and neighborhoods in order to be home. Wherever those we love are, there it is.

We do not ask for what useful purpose
the birds do sing,
for song is their pleasure —
since they were created for singing.
                            —Johannes Kepler

Chapter Nine

Things I Have Learned
from My Children

Children have a refreshing way of looking at things, and many of the lessons I have learned as a mother have come from them, often in unexpected ways.

Lesson One: The Blocks

We had moved to Connecticut and were building a house. In the meantime we were living in a rented house, with furniture and packing boxes stacked in the rooms and garage. It was a complicated time, with children in several different schools and needing chauffeuring at varying hours of the day, and with the house under construction.

Our oldest son, Charles, who had graduated a semester early from high school, had come to us and asked if he could work for our contractor on the construction of the house. Then he could feel that it was truly his home, even though he would be leaving soon for college.

My tentative grip on household organization slipped further and further as the weeks went by. Things that normally seemed simple to me, such as getting the dishes done, the beds made, and the laundry folded, were suddenly monumental tasks that had to be sandwiched between endless errands, and unexpected demands. I felt as if nothing was under control. In the confusion I began to lose motivation and let things slide.

My son came home every day for lunch. Sometimes he would have to fix his own, for I was often driving back and forth to the various schools, or out looking at hardware for the new cabinets. This made me feel cheated, since I knew these few precious weeks were the last weeks I would have this wonderful young man at home.

One day I dashed in the door, with two of the younger children in tow, and saw him just finishing the peanut butter sandwich and milk he had fixed for himself. I had left the kitchen a mess. I hadn't even had time to finish the breakfast dishes, and the makings from the school lunches were still spread over the counters. It was demeaning to me to look at so much evidence that I was not handling my life well.

I sat down next to Charles with a sigh and asked,

"Charles, do you think I've changed? I mean, as I'm getting older, do you think my personality is changing? I feel like I'm a different person."

For a moment Charles thought and then he looked me straight in the eye and said, "No, I don't think you're a different person. You see, I have this theory that everybody is born with a whole set of 'blocks' in their personalities—all different colors and shapes—but they each have their own individual set, and it's theirs for a lifetime. Then, as we live, we shape those blocks into a certain pattern, and for a time that pattern is fairly stable. Then something comes along, like adolescence, or graduation, or a mission—some big change—and it's as if all of our blocks get knocked down, and we have to build up our 'personhood' again.

"In a sense," he added, "I guess we change, because we usually build a new pattern—and maybe a new block comes out on top. But we are still building with the same basic blocks. So, in answer to your question, Mother, I don't think you've basically changed. I just think someone has knocked down your blocks."

Light from this window:

Times of change and upheaval are invaluable. They give us a chance to redesign our blocks.

Lesson Two: The Cookies

I used to triple the cookie dough recipes, and it would take me a whole afternoon to bake the cookies. I would keep both ovens busy, putting in double cookie sheets, then removing the sheets, taking off the hot cookies, forming the new cookies, placing them on the sheets, and putting the next batch on to cook.

One day I asked Catherine, who was about thirteen years old, if she would bake the cookies since I had to go visiting teaching. She was happy to accept the assignment. I left her with a huge batch of dough and expected I would be home before she had finished even half of it.

When I returned, I was amazed to see the table, lined with fresh dish towels. Perfect cookies, beautifully arranged, cooled along its entire expanse. I was astonished at how quickly she had moved the cookies through the process! I watched and soon discovered how she had cut the time of the task in half.

As sheets of cookies baked in the oven (a time during which I fidgeted or was pulled away on another task — often burning the cookies because of lack of attention), Catherine placed waxed paper on the counters and busily spooned out the dough into cookie portions. The minute a sheet of cookies was removed from the oven and the baked cookies were removed from the sheet, she simply picked up the pre-formed cookies, placed them quickly on the sheet, and returned it to the oven. There was no time delay at all. She had the four cookie sheets rotating constantly, and her own time was continuously and effectively used.

Watching the simplicity of her solution and the smoothness and efficiency with which she completed her task, I knew I had not only learned how to bake cookies more efficiently, but I had also learned a principle upon which to base my approach to all habitual tasks.

Light from this window:

Almost every task we do can be done more efficiently if we will give it fresh, analytical, and creative thought.

Lesson Three: The Chair

I walked into the family room at four o'clock, the end of a busy afternoon. It was almost time to start preparing supper, the baby would need attention, and in an hour I had to pick up Charles from his friend's house.

The family room was a mess. Toys were scattered widely, and the floor needed vacuuming desperately. There was just enough time to accomplish the task. But I took a second look and sighed. Somehow the job seemed more than I could do. On a whim I walked across the room, sat down in the armchair, and stared at the disarray.

Just then my five-year-old daughter came through the door and crossed the room on the way to the stairs, heading for her bedroom with an armload of papers and crayons. Her sisters were playing school upstairs. Intent on her errand, she walked right past me. Then, with one foot on the stairway, she whirled around and came back and stood in front of me. Our faces were level with one another, and she looked me directly in the eye. "Mother!" she exclaimed. "What are you doing sitting down?"

The question startled me, and I answered facetiously, "Wishing I had a maid."

She did not laugh. She cocked her head to one side, very seriously, and climbed up on the arm of my chair. "Would you *really* like to have a maid?" she asked.

I remember with such pleasure the conversation that followed. We sat and talked deeply, seriously, about housework, about my feelings toward my home and children, about work itself, about the concept of others working *for* us or *with* us.

After a few minutes she reached over and kissed me and said her sisters were waiting for her upstairs. As I watched her go, I thought with pleasure, "I not only have a daughter, I have just discovered a friend in my own house."

Light from this window:

Let your children see you sitting down once in a while. You are much more approachable. Amazing things can happen when you become still.

Lesson Four: The Letter

Dearest Marianna:

You are three years old today, almost four, and I have just given you permission, for the first time, to walk down our lane to your friend's house, five doors from ours.

The weather is cold. It is March, and, although most of the snow is gone, it has rained this morning, and there are some icy puddles of water in the lane.

When the phone call came inviting you to come for lunch, we went up to your room and you chose your favorite dress to wear. I wonder if you will remember it. It was a rich brown cotton print, with tiny roses on it, and a pretty lace collar. You put on white tights and the fluffy white crinoline that makes your dress puff out from its wide-bowed waistband. I had just polished your little white Mary Jane shoes, and you wanted to wear those too. Then we put on your warm red coat and your white hat with the pom-pom. As I put the mittens on your hands, I thought how small and sweet they are. Your golden hair curls down your back and is almost long enough to reach the hem of your coat.

How dear you are to me! I am very worried about you walking to the neighbors' alone. But no cars are allowed in the lane, and each of the townhouses of Holden Green has its own door and stoop, so you have only to walk past five familiar doors and knock on your friend's house. They are watching for you.

Still, it is very hard for me to let you go on your own. I wouldn't do it except that the baby is very sick, and I cannot take her outside. Over and over again I explained what you must do, and then I kissed you good-bye. The last thing I said was, "Your shoes are so white and clean. Please don't walk in the water and get them muddy."

The minute you left the door, I hurried to the window to watch until I could see you safely into your friend's door. You had no idea that I was watching. You truly thought you were alone — on your own — and so you were. But I was watching, loving you, thinking how dear and precious and wonderful you are, praying that all would go well.

At the first puddle you paused, and I saw you looking at it with yearning eyes. Such a lovely puddle! So perfect for splashing! I was certain that my last admonition would be completely forgotten.

Then I saw the most wonderful thing. With meticulous care you skirted the puddle. On down the lane, with dozens of puddles — big ones, small ones, irregular ones — you zigzagged, skipped, walked sideways, tiptoed, did everything humanly possible to see that not one drop of water touched your polished shoes.

Never realizing you were being watched, you took your first step toward true independence. By your own choice, you obeyed with full heart the things you had been taught.

As I watched you, my heart nearly broke with love, admiration, and tenderness. And I thought that I must write this story down for you and give it to you now, on your sixteenth birthday.

You have become a beautiful young woman. As you continue your journey toward independence, as you begin to date young men and to prepare yourself for the great possibilities of your life, I hope that you will remember the little girl you once were and will follow her example. There will be many puddles and pitfalls that will tempt you, but if you will follow the teachings of the gospel and the guidance of those who love you, and remember those guidelines, even when you think that no one is watching, that no one cares, you will arrive at your destination unspotted from the world.

You can do it, Marianna, for I saw you do it once, as a cherished, wise, and obedient three-year-old.

Thank you for the example, and joy you have been to me.

Love, Mother

Light from this window:

Keep the records of your life. For you and your family they become your own personal scriptures.

A noble type of good,
Heroic womanhood.
— Henry Wadsworth Longfellow

Chapter Ten

Valuing and Understanding Womanhood

One of my favorite quotations is John Locke's wonderful statement, "We are standing on the shoulders of giants." If we had any means by which we could see into our very being—the essence of our cells, the fiber of our spirits, the mysterious veils of emotions, talents, and memory— we might see the wonder of our own personal heritage from all the splendid men and women who created the genetic, spiritual, and cultural matrix from which we— each expressly unique and wonderfully individual—have sprung.

My brother, Thomas Asplund, in his poetic essay "The Heart of My Father," wrote these words: "Who knows what an electronic microscope might do to the great gulf fixed between faith and knowledge? I suppose that one day some chemical mechanic under the flickering death of fluorescent tubes will find deep within the coiling chemistry of my island body a germ of that narrow dirt road which ran through summer's miasma of sweet clover between a beaten windbreak of dusty cottonwoods and in irrigation ditch where once my father ran down tripping ruts of clay in flight and play to the straight gray sanctuary of home."

We all, within the coiling chemistry of our own island bodies, carry the fragrances of other lands, the mysterious heritage of a past that is not our own, but that has been bequeathed to us. To understand the importance of this eternal link between past and future is to understand ourselves better.

In *Time* not long ago, an announcement was made of a newly formed task force whose purpose is to discover the secrets of DNA, to encipher the molecular codes from the past that dwell in the substance of our bodies. The doctor in charge of the research team, Norton Zinder, a molecular biologist, addressed the research team in Washington, D.C., during the opening meeting at the National Institutes of Health. He began his remarks with these words: "Today we begin. We are initiating an unending study of human biology. Whatever it is going to be, it will be an adventure, a priceless endeavor. And when it is done, someone else will sit down and say, 'It is time to begin . . .' "

In his ode "Intimations of Immortality," Wordsworth expressed this thought of each stage of our future and past being linked. He recognized that we spring from a past that we hardly know and little understand, but one that shapes and enriches us:

> Our birth is but a sleep and a forgetting;
> The soul that rises with us, our life's star,
> Hath had elsewhere its setting,
> And cometh from afar:
> Not in entire forgetfulness,
> And not in utter nakedness,
> But trailing clouds of glory do we come
> From God, who is our home.

Then Wordsworth added another line, one that is seldom quoted: "Heaven lies about us in our infancy!"

We are heirs to more than we can possibly dream. I see us as beings of a noble birthright—not clothed in aprons, housecoats, sweaters, or suits and skirts, but trailing invisible streams of majesty, sacrifice, and beauty, the gifts of others that enrobe our spirits, though we are unaware. As T. S. Eliot said, "In our beginning is our end."

The brilliant Irish poet William Butler Yeats developed an entire philosophy of life based upon the concept of the interrelationship of the past to the future. He called it the "gyres" of life. I love that concept because a gyre is not just a circle—it is an upward spiral, a spring. The idea of our lives as the moving point at the end of a gyre is a glorious image. It says that our heritage, our past experiences, the accumulation of learning and knowledge is not a weight to hold us down, but a springboard from which we move to our tomorrows with strength, courage, knowledge, and insight. We may learn to use the patterns of our personal history in that vital way: to propel us into our future.

In *Out of Africa,* Isak Dinesen recalled an incident that occurred when Denys Finch-Hatton showed her his airplane and took her on her first flight. As they soared above the farm, the veldt, and the escarpment where she had lived for sixteen years, she looked down upon her farm, her cherished familiar terrain, and said, with wonder and discovery, "Yes, I see."

How often in our lives do we, like the poets, prophets, philosophers, and scientists, need to look at the great and grand design of our own being, to step away from the dailyness and lift ourselves high enough above our life to see its patterns? Yearning to understand, we see beyond the limited borders of ordinary activities to comprehend something of the sweep of our existence, the noble possibilities in minor, simple things. In that search for understanding we may say, for one brief moment, "Ah, yes, I see."

This overview of our lives allows us to follow the admonition of Matthew Arnold, to see life "steadily, and see it whole." As women, we are so frequently entangled in the demanding tasks at hand, dealing steadily with each subsequent challenge, that we forget to step away occasionally to contemplate, study, reevaluate, and comprehend what we are doing and what are the larger purposes of our ordinary labors.

In searching for this deeper understanding both of our own lives and of the lives of those to whom we are joined by a limitless chain, we need to strive for three things:

1. To better value and understand the nature and privileges of womanhood.

2. To seek greater knowledge of the past and our debt to it — and be more conscious of keeping that knowledge alive.

3. To use our knowledge to make better decisions about the direction of our own future.

In this chapter and the two chapters that follow, we will consider each of these concepts.

The Nature and Privileges of Womanhood

Our generation has lived through one of the most difficult of times for women. The irony is that it is women themselves who have questioned their roles, their worth, and their identity. It is rather like the Utopian Society, which decided that nothing should have material worth and so took gold, the most precious substance, and made chamber pots out of it to destroy its value.

When I was a Beehive Girl in the Mutual Improvement Association, we used to repeat each week this motto: "Taste the sweetness of service; honor womanhood; feel joy."

I believe it is a magnificent thing to be a woman. I have felt that from the time I was about five years old and watched my mother getting ready to go to the stake Gold and Green Ball. Mother was the stake YWMIA president and had helped to decorate the stake cultural hall, manage myriad details, and organize a corps of workers. Now she had a few precious minutes to get ready for the event.

As she put on the last touches of her makeup, I lay on her bed on my stomach and watched her. She was wearing a black satin evening gown with huge puffed sleeves and a sweetheart neckline. I remember the rhinestone pavé clips she placed on either side of the neckline. Her hair was black and shining, and she smelled of perfume and powder.

Last of all she went into her closet and brought out some delicate silver sandals with slender high heels. They looked like something from a fairy tale. We used to play in the back of Mother's closet (we liked the way it smelled, like a hidden garden with roses and lily-of-the-valley). I had seen the beautiful shoes in their special box many times, but I had never seen my mother wear them.

Right then and there, as she put on the magic shoes, I knew what a wonderful thing it was to be a woman. And when my father walked in, wearing a tuxedo (in Canada, the Gold and Green Ball was a formal event), and I saw him smile at my mother with his eyes shining with wonder and love—why, I just knew it was a splendid thing to be a woman.

My feelings remain the same today, after twelve children (eight of them daughters) and all the challenges of a long, complicated, and surprise-filled life. I believe more than ever that it is a splendid thing to be a woman—but now I comprehend that it means far, far more than perfume and silver slippers.

Since our womanhood is an absolutely intrinsic part of our being, loving ourselves requires that we also cherish the nature of our womanhood. The corollary is that the more we love and appreciate womanhood, the easier it is for us to love ourselves.

At the time my husband completed his graduate studies at Harvard, we were surrounded by the new voices of feminism. Anger, frustration, rejection of the past, and denial of the reality and nature of women were hallmarks of much of the rhetoric. I recognized and sympathized with individual pain, and yet I knew that the fundamental and eternal nature of womanhood had great significance and could not be ignored or denied.

One of the things that has helped me to remain fixed in this concept of loving being a woman has been my growing awareness, through study and experience, of how much women are loved, respected, valued, and entrusted by the Lord.

In a wonderful film on the book of Luke, a sensitive actress portrayed the role of Mary with great humility and tenderness. As she walked up the dusty streets of the actual town of Nazareth, I recalled my own visit to that village, and I understood why Phillip had said, with such irony, "Can any good thing come out of Nazareth?" It is hard to explain the obscurity of that spot, and even more difficult to consider that Mary, a young woman living in a simple, agrarian society, was the first being on the earth to know that the time had come when the Savior was about to begin his advent upon the earth.

What a glorious thing it is for a woman to comprehend: that through the power to bear children we are given such a direct link to our Heavenly Father, and that through personal revelation, we will be taught and blessed. As I contemplate this thought, the relationship of the Savior to women becomes more and more fascinating to me. I think of Elisabeth, who carried the great "Elias," John, and who felt the babe within her leap when Mary, pregnant with Jesus, entered the door. I love to read the scriptures, which testify of the great rejoicing, spiritual comprehension, and strength of these mighty women.

My thoughts turn next to Mary and Martha, who, through their womanly care, offered Jesus solace, food, companionship, and a place of rest. How he loved them and sought their company! And they, in turn, learned at his feet and strove to understand his powerful message — and succeeded in doing so to a remarkable degree. Their faith was such that they never even questioned that he could raise their brother, Lazarus, from the dead.

I think of Mary Magdalene, the first being privileged to see the risen Lord. I contemplate the courage of Mary the mother of James, in whose house the early Christians met — at the peril of death. I think of Dorcas, the elderly woman — not beautiful, rich, or powerful — who lovingly sewed coats for the people of her village. When she died, the entire village mourned and sent for Peter, who raised her from the dead. Just a woman, doing "womanly things," and yet considered one of the great.

I think of how Paul counseled Timothy that if he desired to know how to live righteously, he need only follow the examples of his mother and grandmother, for Paul considered them to be the most valiant of righteous beings — examples for all, both male and female.

I think of Mother Eve and how, when Adam came to her to explain the things the Lord had revealed to him about mortality, Eve responded with some of the greatest scriptural wisdom, which elucidated the doctrine of "opposition in all things." And I think of how she, with courage, joy, and humility, and shoulder to shoulder with Adam, prepared to face the coming challenges with a largeness of spirit that we, all her daughters, should yearn to inherit.

That kind of joyous, emotional response, which is one of the great gifts of womanhood, also affected the dear little serving-maid, Rhoda, who, while hiding with the Christians, with Peter in prison and all of them fearing that he might be put to death, heard a rap on the door. She crept to the door, opened it, and discovered Peter, miraculously escaped from prison. Her joy and delight were so overwhelming that she closed the door on Peter and ran to tell the others he was there. They did not believe her news and asked her where he was. Then she realized she had left him on the doorstep, and someone had to run to unlatch the door and let him in. I understand Rhoda. That's why I love being a woman.

My great-grandmother, after rearing eleven children of her own, trained as a midwife and went with her husband to the open prairies of Canada with the first settlers sent by The Church of Jesus Christ of Latter-day Saints.

In the following years she delivered over one thousand babies, and she never lost a baby or a mother. In her old age she retired from the profession but told her cherished granddaughter, my aunt, that she would attend her when she had her first baby.

As the time of her granddaughter's delivery drew near, Grandmother dreamed one night that she was in a bedroom and a woman was having a baby. She walked to the bed, but as she examined the woman, she realized that several things were wrong with the delivery, any one of which could cause death to the mother and the child. She had never, in all of her years of experience, seen a delivery like this, and she had never heard one discussed. She drew back in fear. "I will lose the mother, or the baby, or both," she whispered.

Then the room was filled with light and a voice behind her said, "Proceed with the delivery, and do everything just as I tell you." Slowly and carefully the voice directed her actions, and at last, exhausted but triumphant, she delivered a healthy baby and placed it in the mother's arms.

She awoke with the dream still vivid on her mind. Before the day was over my aunt had gone into labor, and when Grandmother arrived at her bedside, it was exactly the medical presentation she had seen in her dream. The voice of the heavenly messenger still rang in her mind, and she carefully followed his directions, and both the mother and infant lived.

I testify that the Lord loves women. He watches over us and loves our womanhood—the duties and the responsibilities of our gender—and he can speak to us directly with spiritual messages that are necessary for our personal welfare and for the callings in which we are engaged.

Within the purview of the things for which we are responsible—in the clasped network of sisterhood, in unselfish love, nurturing, intellectual growth, joyous energy, and gifts of talent—within the emotional, cultural, and literal bed of womanhood, are created those things which are cherished by society. The rewards of society, the things on which any satisfying society rests, humanity, family, education, love, order, and nests are contained within our errand from the Lord.

Light from this window:

Womanhood is the great mystery, adventure—and endless possibility.

The drift of pinions, would we hearken,
Beats at our own clay-shuttered doors.
—Francis Thompson

Chapter Eleven

The Desire to Know More

An understanding of the relationship between our heritage and ourselves gives us the desire to know more about the past and our debt to it. We need to comprehend the responsibility to gain this knowledge and pass it to others.

A few years ago I was driving my mother from our home in Connecticut to John F. Kennedy Airport on Long Island, New York. In order to get to the airport you must cross the Whitestone Bridge. At the apex of the bridge span is a magnificent view down the East River to the tip of Manhattan Island. A dozen bridges span the river, and the graceful towers of that beautiful city rise against the sky. I relish that view and always gaze at it as I cross the bridge.

My mother, however, was not looking at the view. She was staring speculatively at the intricate, vaulted trusswork of the bridge that spanned the sky over our heads. "My goodness," she murmured, "we have no comprehension of the debts we owe."

Brought back from the view, I looked at her with puzzlement. "What on earth are you talking about?" I asked.

"I'm talking about this bridge," she said. "Do you realize that we drive over this mighty structure without a thought? Who made it? What sacrifices and creativity were involved? What did each individual contribute? And . . . is it safe?"

We laughed at the progression of the questions, but she made me think about how casual we are about the debts we owe to others who have left the work of their hands and minds to enrich our lives.

Living for many years on the East Coast was a privilege in that it developed in me and in my children a lively sense of interest in the historic heritage of our nation. The intellectual heritage represented by libraries; the spiritual heritage by scriptures, journals, and church buildings; the family heritage in records, places, pictures, and inheritances; the unknown heritage of roads, bridges, trails, and cities. Maps, atlases, dictionaries, computers, television, radio, cars — all the heritage of those who have gone before.

Pursuing that thought, I decided to make a study of

the Brooklyn Bridge in the year of the Bridge's Centennial. What incredible things I learned.

The Brooklyn Bridge was built by the Roebling family. The father, John, was a German immigrant who developed the concept of wire-rope or cable, an invention that was necessary for the design of suspension bridges because it was essential to have a support system made of flexible strands that could support tremendous weights.

In the first months of work on the bridge, John Roebling was standing on the dock when a ferry came up to the pier and crushed his foot. He believed in hydrotherapy and thought water could cure anything, so each day he bathed the foot in plain water and drank gallons of water. And he died a cruel death of tetanus.

After his death his son, Washington Augustus, took over the construction of the bridge. Shortly afterwards, he went down in a caisson one day to inspect the pilings. People did not understand the bends in those days, and so he was brought up too quickly and was disabled with what was called caisson disease. Nitrogen had invaded his joints, nervous system, and brain.

For the remainder of the time the bridge was being built, Washington remained in his apartment, which overlooked the building site, and watched progress on the bridge through a telescope by the window. From this vantage point he made suggestions, which his wife wrote down and took to the foreman. In reality, his wife was the moving force. Many people have speculated that the direction and ideas might have been her own, since Washington was so badly disabled.

The story is fraught with drama, tragedy, and heroism,

and the bridge itself is like a cathedral, with its great Gothic stone columns and graceful necklaces of cables. A splendid walkway above the traffic lanes allows people to stroll or jog along the mile-long span, floating in the air high above the wide expanse of the East River. Such a legacy! And so symbolic of all the bridges left for us to cross and climb and reach new places.

The burden—and joy—of the past is that we must preserve it, learn from it, glean from it, and pass it on to the next generation.

As we prepared to celebrate the birthday of Relief Society one year, I recommended that the sego lily be used as our symbol. One of the younger women on the committee looked confused and asked, "What's a sego lily, and why should we use it for this?" She had never heard the story of the sego lilies and the role they played in feeding the starving Saints in the early days of the Church in Utah.

In our families these stories should be known, told, and retold. One of my favorite stories of family heritage is a story of my grandmother, who was deathly afraid of water. Her own mother had drowned, and Grandmother had never learned to swim.

My grandparents, William and Ellen Russell, lived in Provo, Utah. In those days a steamship took people on excursions across Utah Lake for a day of picnicking and fun; however, the lake was so shallow that passengers had to go out to the boat in a dinghy. One day my grandparents, with their new baby, decided to take one of these excursions. That day Grandmother wore a large hat, held on with netting, and a long white dress, with embroidery and a high, stiff lace collar. She was young, slender, beautiful — and very worried about going on a boat. Carrying her baby, who was also dressed in a long white dress, she was lifted from the dock to the dinghy that would take them out to the steam paddler. As she was arranging her skirt to sit down, another passenger stepped into the boat and Grandmother lost her balance. Still holding the baby, she fell over backwards into the water, which was over her head.

Instantly Grandfather and some other men lifted her out of the lake, back onto the dock. Dripping wet and in total shock, she stood on the dock, speechless. Someone tried to take the baby away so that they could towel her and the baby off, but they could not pry the baby out of her arms. Finally Grandfather gently loosened her hold and took the baby in his arms. The amazing thing was that Grandma had held the baby so closely and so protectively that the front of her dress was *bone dry*. Such love! What a wonderful heritage!

My husband's grandmother, Anna Rhodelia, was left a widow at the age of twenty-one. She had two little boys under the age of three and a third one was born four months after her husband's death. The family was destitute, living in a small log cabin and with no close relatives or friends.

When Anna's baby was born, Anna became terribly ill. She had a raging fever, had lost a great deal of blood, and was clinging to life by a thread. A few relatives who visited her, seeing her in what they thought was a comatose state, began reluctantly to decide who should raise the children. None of them could take all three. Listening to them, Anna felt a great fire building within her, and she spoke directly to the Lord. "You have taken my mother and my father. You have taken my brothers and sisters. You have taken my husband. You must not take me. I must be allowed to live and raise my sons. I will not let them be raised without love—without one another."

Miraculously Anna rose from her death bed and, through years of incredible sacrifice and work, managed to raise her three sons.

Within womanhood is magnificent spiritual power. We are descended from women who understood that power, and we must learn about them and teach their stories to our children.

America's Secret Aristocracy by Stephen Birmingham is a fascinating chronicle of some of the oldest, most aristocratic families of America, families that have quietly amassed and used power and wealth. These families form an unpublicized and private network, with subtle (and some not-so-subtle) speech patterns, mores, and social traditions. (Parenthetically, most Mormons would understand such cultural subtleties. We recognize a number of them in our own infrastructure.)

As I read the book, it was interesting to note that one of the traditions that keeps these aristocratic families cohesive is that they have a pattern of remembering their ancestry. Their homes are filled with family portraits, heirlooms, mementos of the past, and photographs. Their conversation is peppered with reference to their ancestors—eccentric, respected, and impressive men and women. Children are taught that the family's past is part of their present.

This is an example we should follow. As women we have a unique, vibrant, and rich heritage that must be preserved. We should weave it into our daily lives and teach it to our children. It is the gold that we should garner from the ashes.

I recently researched the life of the first Mormon woman in Dallas. Eliza was converted by missionaries in Rockwall, a small community about thirty miles east of Dallas. At seventeen she married a neighbor's son, whom she fell in love with at first sight.

Eliza tells in her journal of the struggle she and Kelsey had to support themselves on a poor cotton farm. She described how she gave birth to her third baby without anyone in attendance except Kelsey (who had no idea what to do) after a full day of labor picking cotton in the heat of the Texas summer.

How Eliza loved the gospel! When she and Kelsey finally decided they must move to Dallas to find work, she wept all the way, feeling she was going to the ends of the earth. On the wagon trip, she took a pile of church tracts and dropped them from the wagon as they traveled, leaving a trail of "missionary opportunities" from Rockwall to Dallas. She prayed people would find the pamphlets on the road, pick them up, read them, and then search out the Church. I think, too, that she left the tracts like Hansel and Gretel left the bread crumbs, hoping perhaps someday she could follow them back to Rockwall.

The first tiny church meetings in Dallas were held in Eliza's home. She has lived to see seven stakes organized in Dallas, and her own beloved grandson, Floyd Humphries, was the architect of the Dallas Temple.

In women such as Eliza, we see the patterns of aspiring to grow, yearning to know more, and bequeathing a meaningful legacy.

Light from this window:

We are the bridge over which the next generation will cross from the past to the future.

Out of our . . . lineage, minds will spring
that will reach back to us . . . to know us
better than we know ourselves. [They] shall
stand upon this earth . . . and shall laugh
and reach out their hands amidst the stars.

— H. G. Wells

Chapter Twelve

Building Our Tomorrows

Marley's ghost came to Scrooge with the symbols of
his past clanging like cymbals around him — weighted,
chained, burdened by past mistakes, omissions, false
goals, and desires. Too often this is our view of our own
past, and it creates prisons of self-doubt, old habits, and
childhood perceptions of our own limitations and flaws.

The reality is, however, that when his past became
real to Marley, when he truly understood it, for the first
time he had the opportunity to become free. If he had

remained ignorant of it, he would have remained unchanged. Knowledge became for him the means of salvation, and the means for the salvation of others, too.

With an understanding of our own past, each of us may start where we are and build our future on solid foundations. First we must learn to remember the good things, to forgive others, and to forgive ourselves for past error. We must view the little child within us with love, compassion, and understanding for past mistakes and trials.

If something in our personal past is amiss, we should face it clearly. If we have repented, we should forget; if it was a wrong, we should forgive; if it is something requiring repentance, we should get about the task of doing so—and repent with joy and gratitude for that window which allows us to use even the mistakes of the past an opportunity to grow. In his inaugural address in January 1989, President George Bush quoted a phrase that goes something like this: "Though our flaws may be endless, God's love is bounteous." We must believe in forgiveness as much as we believe in love.

In our building of our own future, we should choose those things from our past that will build and lift us up. The stumbling block of despair and discontent occurs when we perceive that we have become powerless—powerless to change; powerless to do; powerless to be happy; powerless to lift our spirits. The one thing we as Latter-day Saint women must know, without question, is that no one can rob us of our free agency. It is a divinely given gift. We, and we alone, can rob ourselves of that attribute given to us by our Heavenly Father.

Terry Anderson was a hostage in captivity in Beirut for five years. Though he was imprisoned all that time in a dark cell, he was able to keep his mind and spirit strong. Another prisoner who was placed briefly in the same room with Terry recounted how Terry had lifted his spirits and told him over and over again, "Do not lose courage."

Life can constrain us in ways that seem as difficult as a prison, but our will remains free, and we have control over how we will act and feel. We must not lose courage. All this is for our own good. The blessings will come.

Many people say things like "Seize the day!" "Live life to the fullest!" and, instead of making us feel eager, the words make us feel overwhelmed. We feel we don't have any day to seize — it is all used up with obligations and tasks. But the secret to enjoying those obligations is to seize control, to seize the obligations and the tasks and see them as things we have chosen to do, and then to do them in the ways we choose.

Each of us can find ways to measure even the smallest accomplishments. The joyous vantage point is to envision our own spiral and to see ourselves each day gradually building upon that and moving upward. The pace is absolutely our own, the direction is our own. As we see ourselves moving forward, feeling our past firmly beneath us, we can then go forth with faith and relish our own individuality.

Once we have begun to spiral upward, we need to watch for stumbling blocks from our past life. The best signal is when we feel unrest in our hearts. I believe that unrest of the heart is the impression of the Holy Ghost guiding us to something that must be resolved before we can move forward again. Rather than fearing unease or avoiding it, we can search it out and use it to discover what is troubling us. Then we should pray and ask the Lord to help us solve it. We should use our own wisdom, garnered from our past experiences and our own knowledge. If necessary, we can consult with friends or advisers. Then we can act—change direction, apologize, move, learn, study, or enliven, whatever the need is.

As we look into our past, we will find, surprisingly, courage and resources that we never dreamed we had. The important thing is not to allow our past to place limitations on us or discourage us. That is not the purpose of experience.

Lillian Gilbreth, whose story is told in the book *Cheaper by the Dozen* and the play of the same name, was born to a wealthy California family in the last decade of the nineteenth century. As a child, she was so painfully shy that she was incapable of attending school. Each year her parents enrolled her in school, but after a few days of her suffering they would allow her to remain at home with a tutor. Finally she was able to return to high school to complete her education.

At the turn of the century it was rare for young women to attend college, but Lillian had such a passion for knowledge that she convinced her parents to allow her to attend the University of California. Though she was tall and slender, she was still enormously shy and carried herself in a slightly hunched posture, with her head down.

But Lillian had great strength of will when it came to doing something she felt was right. And so, when she was the top graduate of her class and therefore eligible to be the valedictorian, she rose above her natural diffidence and determined to fulfill that role. The president of the university was uncomfortable with having a woman speak to a mixed assembly, so he gave her some strict instructions: She could speak—he couldn't deny her that privilege—but she must wear something frilly around the collar of her robe, wear her hair in a very feminine style, use no hand gestures, and read her talk from small notecards. "Nothing in your manner or deportment should suggest you are trying to appear like a man," he decreed.

Soon after her graduation, while on her way to Europe, Lillian met and fell in love with a charismatic whirlwind of a man, Frank Gilbreth. Though he had a scanty education, he had discovered a whole new field of engineering—time management. He swept her off her feet and they were soon married. This catapulted her into a world of a new baby every year, a domineering mother-in-law, and, eventually, a huge house in New Jersey, filled with eleven children (one child died in infancy). The Gilbreths had servants to do the cooking and cleaning, which was a blessing because Lillian did not know how to cook—and, indeed, never learned. She spent her days interacting, primarily one on one, with her children, and serving as a behind-the-scenes adviser, consultant, and ghost writer for her husband. She also obtained a doctorate, but in those years her life remained very private and constrained.

In 1924 Frank was invited to attend a worldwide conference of engineers. He called Lillian from the train station, and while they were speaking he collapsed and died. At age forty-seven, Lillian was left alone, with very little money, to raise a huge family.

But her past was her prologue. And while the most visible thing in her personality for years had been her shyness and her shrinking from public interchange, that part of her past had to be ignored and forgotten. The other part of her past — the courage, the stubbornness, the love of her children, her brilliant intellect, and the knowledge she had gained of her husband's work — *those* were the things from her past that she drew from and on which she built her next thirty years.

After organizing her children and her household, she began a career in a field dominated by men. She convinced the major clients of Frank's company that she could perform the services for which they had hired her husband. She also held training seminars in her own home, and gradually she gained the whole-hearted admiration and respect of the engineering community. She became, in her own right, one of the most celebrated time-management engineers in the world. Even into her seventies she fulfilled scores of speaking engagements throughout the world each year. Although she herself never learned to use a kitchen, we benefit from her vision of what a kitchen should be. The style of cabinetry and design of applicances and lighting in our modern kitchens are a result largely of her research.

What a great lesson! We must not let our past limit us. Within it are the clues to our own personal possibilities.

Lastly, as we build our future, the timeless structures of the gospel can give us confidence and a sense of peace.

So often we want to make life more complex than it really is. My husband has set a powerful example in this. Whenever my life seems shaken and unfocused, I know the rock upon which to stand to bring back order. This rock includes personal prayer every morning and evening, scripture reading every day, and journal keeping.

In the movie *How Green Was My Valley* is a scene that takes place at the Welsh mining family's dinner table. At the head of the table the father listens in anguish as his four grown sons declare their fury at the coal mine owners, and they leave the table to pack their things to go to America. The heartbroken father remains in the darkened room with his head bowed. At the far end of the table the youngest son sits in silence, looking lovingly at his father. Finally he clears his throat so his father will notice him. Without raising his head the father says tenderly, "Yes, my son, I know you are there."

And that, ultimately, is the greatest measure of our past and our future—that we are where the Lord would have us be, where we are needed and expected, and where we desire to be. How I admire the women of the Church who stand upon the mark. "Yes, my daughters," our Heavenly Father says, "I know you are there."

And so we continue in that great and glorious enigma of womanhood, at the same time so simple and yet so complex. The past, the present, and the future mingling in our vision; the joys so intense, the sorrows so poignant, and the days so full.

I once saw a little painting at the Museum of Church History and Art in Salt Lake City that depicted a pioneer mother with her two little daughters. The mother and children stand on the prairie in the foreground, with the wagon train making camp in the distance. The long skirts and hair of the woman and girls are windblown. In the sunshine, the little girls are filling their sunbonnets full of the bright sunflowers that dot the prairie. The mother is smiling at them, her face so full of love that it almost hurts to look at her. But the irony is that she has a wooden spade in her hands and is piling buffalo chips into a small wheelbarrow to take back to camp for the evening fire.

As I looked at the picture, so full of beauty, duty, sacrifice, and love, I smiled to myself and thought, "That's exactly what a woman's life is — sunflowers and buffalo chips." I am grateful for a heritage that makes me see these things more clearly.

Light from this window:

A book, a challenge, a friend, a child, a chore, a tale, a word, an act, a moment of stillness, a trial, a blessing, a prayer. All are windows into the light.

> The patient stars
> Lean from their lattices,
> content to wait,
> Wait for the day that maketh
> All things clear.
>
> — Bret Harte